YORK NOTES

Homer
The Odyssey

(Translated by E.V. Rieu; revised by D.C.H. Rieu)

Note by Robin Sowerby

 Longman

York Press

The quotation from James Joyce on p. 7 is by kind permission of Stephen James Joyce.

The Publisher has made every effort to contact copyright holders for any quotations used in the text.

York Press
322 Old Brompton Road, London SW5 9JH

PEARSON EDUCATION LIMITED
Edinburgh Gate, Harlow,
Essex CM20 2JE, United Kingdom
Associated companies, branches and representatives throughout the world

First published 2000
21 20

ISBN 978-0-582-43151-5

Designed by Vicki Pacey
Phototypeset by Gem Graphics, Trenance, Mawgan Porth, Cornwall
Colour reproduction and film output by Spectrum Colour
Printed in China
(CTPS/20)

CONTENTS

PART ONE

INTRODUCTION

HOW TO STUDY AN EPIC NARRATIVE POEM (IN PROSE TRANSLATION)

Studying a long narrative poem on your own requires self-discipline and a carefully thought-out work plan in order to be effective.

- You will need to read the work more than once. Start by reading it quickly for pleasure, then read it slowly and thoroughly.
- On your second reading make detailed notes on the plot, characters and themes. Further readings will generate new ideas.
- Make sure you understand all the mythological references. Look names up in a dictionary if necessary.
- Remember that, though you are reading it in modern prose, the work is from a different culture and time. Make an imaginative effort to read it on its own terms, noting how it differs from modern stories set in the modern world.
- **Epic** poems feature epic heroes. What are the characteristics of heroic behaviour in this work and how do they differ from those exhibited by other heroic figures?
- Think about the way in which the narrative unfolds: the time-scheme and the different settings may be a key to its structure and organisation.
- Are words, images or motifs repeated so as to give the work a pattern? Do such patterns help you to understand the work's themes?
- It is difficult when commenting on a work in translation to make precise points about its style. But think of its style in broad terms, noting such features as the recurring **epithets**, the extended **similes**, the set speeches, the intervention of the divine. Compare with another translation if you can.
- Does the work present a moral and just world?
- Cite exact sources for all quotations. Wherever possible find your own examples from the work to back up your own opinions.
- Always express your ideas in your own words.

This York Note offers an introduction to the *Odyssey* and cannot substitute for close reading of the text and the study of secondary sources.

Homer's *Odyssey*, together with his *Iliad*, stands at the head of the western tradition, not only in time but also as one of the great classic texts in the whole of world literature. And few of the world's great classics have had such an enduring popular appeal. Its title has entered general consciousness as the dignified expression for a great journey. Generations of readers have been enthralled by the tales of the intrepid traveller's encounters with Circe and the Cyclops, the Sirens, the Lotus-eaters, and Scylla and Charybdis. This is the stuff of romance and the story has a romantic ending when, after much suffering and enduring, the returning husband and his loyal and steadfast wife are finally reunited in the poem's emotional climax. Yet, despite the elements of romance, there is more than an undercurrent of gritty realism as Odysseus, in a beggar's disguise, has to use all his cunning to outwit the arrogant and profligate Suitors who have occupied his house in his absence, are wooing his wife and plotting the death of his son. There is much **pathos** and **irony**, as he tests loyalties and endures the Suitors' insults, seeing for himself what is happening and waiting for the opportunity to exact a just vengeance. Throughout, the hero is much suffering but he is also the man of many turns who achieves through his own devices a just triumph over his enemies.

Although it is an **epic**, the *Odyssey* has been variously called an adventure story, a moral tale, the precursor of romance or of **picaresque** fiction, or simply the first realistic novel. This itself indicates the different interests it can satisfy and the rich and varied texture of the poem.

Although it is concentrated upon the very last stages of Odysseus's long journey and may be said to have a domestic theme – the re-establishment of Odysseus as rightful lord in his own house – the poem has a wide scope. The journey of Telemachus to seek news of his father at the beginning takes us to the palaces of Nestor and Menelaus, where we hear of the fortunes of other returning heroes as well as the heroic part played by Odysseus in the great Trojan story. We hear of Agamemnon, Achilles and Ajax when Odysseus speaks to them in Hades and again when the dead Suitors arrive there and tell Agamemnon what has happened to them. Thereupon Agamemnon contrasts the good fortune of Odysseus with his own misfortune, lamenting his death at the hands of his wife Clytemnestra and praising the contrasting virtue of the wife of Odysseus: 'The glory of her virtue will not fade with the years, but the deathless gods themselves will make a beautiful song for mortal ears in honour of the constant Penelope' (Book 24, lines 196–7). This song may be said to be the poem itself, for Penelope no less than Odysseus is long suffering and has had to use her wits to outwit the Suitors.

Still, all depends on the hero, and Odysseus, perhaps the most interesting fictional character in Greek literature, has always captured the imagination of readers. He inspired James Joyce in *Ulysses* (the Roman version of his name).

> 'Your complete man in literature is, I suppose, Ulysses?'
>
> 'Yes,' said Joyce. ... 'No-age Faust isn't a man ... you mentioned Hamlet. Hamlet is a human being, but he is a son only. Ulysses is son to Laertes, but he is father to Telemachus, husband to Penelope, lover of Calypso, companion in arms of the Greek warriors around Troy, and King of Ithaca. He was subjected to many trials, but with wisdom and courage came through them all. ... Another thing, the history of Ulysses did not come to an end when the Trojan War was over. It began just when the other Greek heroes went back to live the rest of their lives in peace. And then –' Joyce laughed – 'he was the first gentleman in Europe. When he advanced, naked, to meet the young princess he hid from her maidenly eyes the parts that mattered of his brinesoaked, barnacle-encrusted body. He was an inventor too. The tank was his creation. Wooden horse or iron box – it doesn't matter. They are both shells containing armed warriors.'
>
> 'What do you mean,' said Budgen, 'by a complete man? For example, if a sculptor makes a figure of a man then that man is all-round, three-dimensional, but not necessarily complete in the sense of being ideal. All human bodies are imperfect, limited in some way, human beings too. Now your Ulysses ...'
>
> 'He is both,' said Joyce. 'I see him from all sides, and therefore he is all-round in the sense of your sculptor's figure. But he is a complete man as well – a good man.'
>
> (Frank Budgen, *James Joyce and the Making of Ulysses*, O.U.P., 1972, quoted in Richard Ellman, *James Joyce*, O.U.P., 1959, pp. 435–6)

The all-round man is indeed a Greek ideal, revived in the Renaissance, and Odysseus in the poem is its first great example, for he represents a blend of the physical and the intellectual and has an appreciation of the artistic. This is most apparent in Phaeacia where he has arrived after his shipwreck. Phaeacia itself is redolent of Greek ideals. The striking description of its beautiful garden and the magnificent palace of the

Phaeacian king (a reminder of the sophisticated monuments of Mycenaean culture) evokes a world of material splendour in which the physical and the artistic are equally valued. In this setting as he is about to set out for the palace, the hero is endowed with a beauty that has come to be regarded as the Greek ideal, gloriously represented on surviving statues:

> Athene ... made him seem taller and sturdier and caused the bushy locks to hang from his head thick as the petals of the hyacinth in bloom. Just as a craftsman trained by Hephaestus and Pallas Athene in the secrets of his art puts a graceful finish to his work by overlaying silverware with gold, she endowed his head and shoulders with beauty. When Odysseus retired to sit down by himself on the sea-shore, he was radiant with grace and beauty. (Book 6, lines 229–35)

Once there, he is entertained with food and drink, with dancing and with the songs of the minstrel. He is then invited to compete in the Phaeacian games by one of the king's sons: 'It is only right that you should be an athlete, for nothing makes a man so famous during his lifetime as what he can achieve with his hands and feet' (Book 8, lines 146–8). He declines, but another Phaeacian assails him with the taunt that he is a mere trader concerned with profit. His heroic spirit responds angrily with the remark that 'the gods do not grace men equally with the attributes of good looks, brains and eloquence' (Book 8, line 168). He then participates and excels, proving himself here the all-round man comprising the Greek ideal.

As he begins the narrative of his tales, he gives voice to a further Homeric ideal in his praise of the feast and the song:

> 'King Alcinous ... it is indeed a lovely thing to hear a bard such as this, with a voice like the voice of the gods. I myself feel that there is nothing more delightful than when the festive mood reigns in the hearts of all the people and the banqueters listen to a minstrel from their seats in the hall, while the tables before them are laden with bread and meat, and a steward carries round the wine he has drawn from the bowl and fills their cups. This, to my way of thinking, is perfection.' (Book 9, lines 1–11)

This Hellenic world is one in which the minstrel (not the priest or the prophet) has the honoured place and where life in the here and now and the representation of it in song are supremely celebrated.

Odysseus as he tells his tale enthrals his audience who are 'Held by the spell of his words' (Book 11, line 333) and honour him with gifts as a consequence. Later Eumaeus gives Penelope this testimony about the stranger in their midst (the disguised Odysseus): 'Sitting in my home he held me spellbound. It was like fixing one's eyes on a minstrel who has been taught by the gods to sing words that bring delight to mortals, and everyone longs to hear him when he sings' (Book 17, lines 518–20). The Homeric singer of tales has made his hero a man after his own heart and there is no more eloquent hero in literature.

The plot of the *Odyssey* requires the hero through his disguise to show presence of mind and restraint. One of the **epithets** given to both Odysseus and Penelope is the Greek word *echephron*, which literally means 'having mind' and is variously translated as 'wise', 'self-possessed', 'having understanding', 'prudent'. Telemachus, too, is said to be *pepnumenos* 'showing understanding'. So many Greek myths show the dominance of cruel and treacherous passions indulged without any restraint of civilised feeling or morality but, in the *Odyssey*, Homer rewards the wise restraint of his characters and serenely celebrates the most basic natural bonds of human life between parent and child and above all between husband and wife. It could be said too that Homer endows them with that quality of restraint that he shows himself in the controlling artistry of his poem, manifested in its unity and balanced structure. The poem may be said to recommend the two great maxims of Greek culture later inscribed on the portal of the temple of Apollo at Delphi: *gnothi seauton*, Know Thyself, and *meden agan*, Nothing in Excess.

But this could be rather dull, if that was all that could be said. There are other ways of looking at the hero and the poem. Part of Odysseus's completeness is that he is not completely ideal. He has some of the defects of his virtues. Some critics have found in him a strain of greedy materialism and a reckless and vainglorious concern with his own reputation that endangers his companions. His slaying of all the Suitors indiscriminately even though he recognises degrees of culpability has been considered a moral defect. He certainly seems to take the testing of loyalty rather far in torturing his poor father after the Suitor-slaying, when it is scarcely necessary. Is he as good as Joyce asserts, or is his 'wisdom' simply self-serving cleverness? Such doubts about the hero have been entertained about the whole poem, principally in comparison to the more heroic *Iliad*. The connections with the heroic past are somewhat distant; the main action concerns domestic affairs and a struggle with ignoble opponents. This struggle forces the king to don the robes of a beggar and to resort to tricks and chicanery that might be deemed unworthy of a noble nature.

PART TWO

COMMENTARIES

There have been many editions of the *Odyssey* since the first edition printed in Florence in 1488. A reliable plain text of the Greek is the Oxford Classical Text of the *Odyssey* edited by T.W. Allen, in two volumes, published by the Clarendon Press, Oxford, 1917. An informative edition of the Greek for students is *The Odyssey of Homer* edited with a general and grammatical introduction, commentary and indexes by W.B. Stanford, in two volumes, published by Macmillan, London, 1948–50.

In the preparation of this Note intended primarily for students reading a translation, the following version has been used: *Homer: The Odyssey*, translated by E.V. Rieu, revised translation by D.C.H. Rieu, with an introduction by Peter Jones, Penguin Books, Harmondsworth, 1991, and reprinted subsequently. This edition has the line numbers of the Greek text at the side of the page. Quotations in this Note are all from the above edition; line numbers, however, refer to the original Greek, so will often differ slightly from this modern translation which is not line by line. It will, nonetheless, be possible to use them with any reasonably close translation. Greek names are given in the form in which they appear in the Penguin translation and in which they are most familiar in English: that is, Achilles, for example, rather than Akilleus, Ajax not Aias and Ithaca not Ithaka.

Most of the place names can be found on the map provided on p. 114 though it should be remembered that identification of place names in Homer is often dubious and frequently a matter of scholarly dispute. Many of the places visited by Odysseus are imaginary and Homer does not always suggest their location in relation to known landmarks so that it is not really possible to pinpoint Odysseus's journey on an actual map with any surety.

The poet introduces the **saga** of Odysseus, the hero who went with the Greeks to Troy and after the ten years' siege was destined to undertake a great journey on which he saw many peoples and had many adventures, in the course of which all his companions perished. The muse begins the tale at the time, just before his final return home to the island of Ithaca, when Odysseus, who has been a prisoner of the nymph Calypso for seven years on the island of Ogygia, is about to be released. In a council of the gods in the absence of Poseidon, who is hostile to Odysseus because he has blinded his son Polyphemus the Cyclops, Athene protests on behalf of her favourite Odysseus and Zeus agrees to send Hermes to order Calypso to allow him to go home. Athene proposes to go to Ithaca herself in order to prompt Telemachus, Odysseus's son, first to call an assembly to denounce the Suitors who are occupying his house and wasting his property while they woo his mother Penelope, and second, to make a journey to Pylos and Sparta in search of news of his father from his old comrades Nestor and Menelaus, who have returned from Troy. This is the subject of Books 1–4, sometimes called the Telemachid or the Telemacheia.

Disguised as a stranger, Athene is welcomed by Telemachus, who explains the situation in the palace to her. His mother is trying to ward off the Suitors' advances out of loyalty to Odysseus. Athene gives her advice. Telemachus asserts himself in dealing with his mother and in proposing an assembly of all the Ithacans for the following day (Book 1).

In the assembly Telemachus denounces the Suitors, but they show no intention of leaving; instead, they complain of Penelope's behaviour and advise him to send her back to her father's house. Telemachus asks for a ship to make his journey. In the palace that night they mock Telemachus but he nevertheless manages to acquire his ship and sets off for Pylos (Book 2). Here he meet Nestor and hears of his father's exploits at Troy and of the return of other Greek heroes from the Trojan campaign. But Nestor knows nothing of Odysseus's present whereabouts (Book 3). Telemachus journeys on to Sparta where he is entertained by Menelaus and Helen who also have reminiscences of his father and the returning Greeks. Menelaus tells of the news he received from the divine prophet Proteus that Odysseus is a prisoner on Calypso's island. Back in Ithaca the Suitors plot to kill Telemachus in an ambush on his return (Book 4).

In a second council of the gods Zeus sends Hermes to tell Calypso to release Odysseus. Odysseus builds a raft and sets sail for Scherie, a journey of twenty days. On the eighteenth day Poseidon, on his return from a visit to the Ethiopians, catches sight of Odysseus, and raises a storm in which he is shipwrecked. Eventually after great difficulty and peril he lands in Scherie (Book 5).

After a night's rest he is awakened by the sound of female voices and encounters Nausicaa, the daughter of King Alcinous of the Phaeacians, who, together with her maids, is washing clothes in an adjacent river. She directs him to the palace and recommends that he petition her mother Queen Arete (Book 6). This he does, asking for passage home. In response to Arete's enquiry he tells of his stay with Calypso and his journey from Ogygia (Book 7). The following day he is entertained by the Phaeacians. There is dancing and song from the bard Demodocus. Games are held in which Odysseus distinguishes himself when provoked into competition by an insult from a young Phaeacian. At the evening banquet Demodocus sings of the Wooden Horse. Noting his tearful reaction Alcinous asks Odysseus to give an account of himself (Book 8).

In reply Odysseus tells of his wanderings from Troy before he reached Calypso's island in a narrative that extends over four books (9–12) called by the ancients 'narratives to Alcinous'. He begins with the sack of Ismarus and the encounter with the Cicones, followed by encounters with the Lotus-eaters and with the Cyclops (Book 9). He then meets Aeolus, the Laestrygonians and Circe who tells him that he must consult Teiresias in Hades (Book 10). Following Circe's instructions he summons up the spirits of the dead and speaks first with Teiresias who tells him not to harm the oxen of the Sun, informs him of trouble at home and prophesies his future, and then Odysseus speaks to his mother Anticleia. There follows the catalogue of famous women. Odysseus then speaks with Agamemnon, Achilles and Ajax, and sees other heroes (Book 11). Circe, to whom he then returns, tells him of dangers to come. He avoids the Wandering Rocks but encounters the Sirens and then Scylla and Charybdis. Finally he reaches Thrinacie where his men kill the oxen of the Sun. They lose their lives when Zeus wrecks their ship with a thunderbolt. Odysseus, the sole survivor, drifts to the island of Ogygia (Book 12).

The Phaeacians escort Odysseus loaded with gifts in one of their magic ships by night to Ithaca. When he wakes up on the Ithacan shore where he had been left asleep he does not recognise the place. Athene in disguise enlightens him. Disguising his own identity Odysseus tells his first Cretan tale. The goddess reveals herself, plans his disguise as a beggar and sets him on the road to the dwelling of Eumaeus his loyal steward (Book 13). Eumaeus welcomes the stranger, who tells his second Cretan tale to conceal his identity (Book 14). Telemachus makes hasty preparations to return home. Odysseus enquires about his father Laertes. Eumaeus tells his own history. Telemachus lands in Ithaca, having evaded the Suitors' plot (Book 15). He arrives at Eumaeus's hut. Odysseus reveals himself to his son and together they plot the Suitors' destruction. The Suitors, realising that Telemachus has escaped, discuss a further plot to ambush him on his return to the palace (Book 16).

The action now moves to the palace. Telemachus sets off first, followed later by Odysseus and Eumaeus. En route Odysseus is insulted by the goatherd Melantheus. He enters the palace and begs from the Suitors. Antinous their leader throws a stool at him (Book 17). He fights with the beggar Irus and is insulted by a maidservant Melantho and by another Suitor Eurymachus (Book 18). He speaks with Penelope and repeats his Cretan history to her. He is washed by his old nurse Eurycleia who recognises him from his scar. She is sworn to secrecy. Penelope announces to the stranger her decision to institute the contest with the bow, with the intention of marrying the winner (Book 19). Odysseus sees the waste of his resources in the preparations being made for a banquet. He is insulted by a Suitor, Ctesippus. The prophet Theoclymenus foresees the Suitors' doom (Book 20). Penelope fetches the bow which the Suitors try but fail to string. Odysseus asks if he may try his hand. Telemachus orders that he be given the bow which he successfully strings, shooting through the twelve axes (Book 21).

Now begins the killing of the Suitors and the re-establishment of Odysseus as master of his own house. Antinous falls first. Odysseus then reveals himself and so commences the general slaughter. The errant maids are hanged and the house fumigated (Book 22). Eurycleia gives the news to Penelope who cannot believe that her husband has returned. After testing him she eventually suspends her disbelief and Odysseus tells her of his wanderings (Book 23). The souls of the Suitors are ushered by

Hermes into Hades where the spirit of Agamemnon asks them what has happened to bring so many of them at once. When Amphimedon tells him, Agamemnon extols Odysseus's action and Penelope's virtue. Odysseus goes to his father's farm for the final recognition scene. The Suitors' relatives, in an assembly, decide to avenge the death of their sons. Laertes, Odysseus and Telemachus commence battle which is stopped by Zeus and Athene who command the peace with which the poem ends (Book 24).

DETAILED COMMENTARIES

BOOK 1   Athene visits Telemachus

See the opening of the synopsis for a summary of this book.

> The proposition or summary of the poem's subject hails Odysseus as the resourceful hero who engineered the sack of Troy (through the device of the Wooden Horse), and as the long-suffering traveller who has seen cities and men. He is distinguished from his followers who lost their return through their own witlessness. It is to be presumed that these lines summarise what Odysseus was famous for in Homer's day, and that their function is simply to bring that famous story to mind, for Homer bids his muse to begin the tale at any point she wishes. In the event, Homer's muse does not make the subject of this proposition the centre of the poem's main action. The loss of Odysseus's comrades, far from being central, is a mere **episode** narrated in little more than 100 lines (Book 12, lines 256–375). Nor is his 'Odyssey' the main subject. The main subject is the hero's return and his re-establishment of order in his own house.

> Zeus's keynote speech, in which he berates men for blaming the gods for their misfortunes when they come to grief through their own transgressions, suggests that this will be a moral tale which will turn on individual moral choice. He makes his point with reference to the fate of Aegisthus who freely chose to act immorally in stealing Agamemnon's wife and was justly punished

by Agamemnon's son Orestes. This prefigures divine support for
Telemachus, Odysseus's son, in asserting his father's rights.

The conversation that follows between Athene and Zeus establishes
three key elements in the relation of the gods to Odysseus in the
poem; he is admired by Zeus who is eager that he return home; he
is the special favourite of Athene who takes practical steps to make
his return possible, and is hated by Poseidon (because he had
blinded his son Polyphemus, the Cyclops) who will continue to
thwart him.

Athene's plan to send Hermes to order Calypso to free Odysseus
and to send Telemachus to Pylos and Sparta in search of his father
initiates the action that is to take place over the next five books.
(Although freely undertaken, human actions in the poem generally
have their origin in divine promptings.) Homer has used the
council of the gods to initiate his plot and to suggest its moral
dimension.

Telemachus's conversation with Athene in the disguise of a stranger
establishes his good manners in contrast to the Suitors' profligate
behaviour, and introduces one of the great ethical imperatives of the
poem, the obligation of hospitality to the stranger. It also
establishes the uncertainty surrounding the fate of Odysseus. Her
tale in answer to Telemachus's question is the first of many tales
within the tale. The disorderly situation in the house of Odysseus is
established dramatically through the conversation between
characters; the goddess's disapproval reinforces the judgement
against the Suitors. Her exhortation that Telemachus must be as
brave as Orestes (line 296) echoes the earlier approval of Zeus for
Orestes's role as the avenger of Agamemnon and suggests that
Telemachus must now assert himself on behalf of his father's rights.

The pathos of the situation is brought out in the suffering of
Penelope who is distressed when she hears the resident bard
entertaining the Suitors (as Homer is entertaining his audience),
by singing of the woes of the Achaeans on their return from Troy.

Telemachus's rebuke to Penelope which takes her by surprise and
his bold altercation with the Suitors demonstrates a crucial new

ingredient in the plot: his new-found confidence, now that he is about to take matters into his own hands, following the advice of Athene.

1 **Muse** goddess of poetry. According to later writers there were nine muses who were the daughters of Zeus and Memory, each presiding over one of the major arts (see also Book 24, line 60)

2 **Troy** the siege of Troy (in Asia Minor), undertaken after the Trojan Paris had abducted the Greek Helen from Sparta, had lasted ten years. The stratagem of the Wooden Horse by which Troy was finally taken was devised by Odysseus (see Book 8, lines 492–520). Menelaus, the husband of Helen, describes Odysseus's crucial role in restraining the Greeks inside the horse from shouting out and revealing their presence (Book 4, lines 266–89)

8 **the oxen of Hyperion** the episode is narrated by Odysseus to the Phaeacians (Book 12, lines 265–375). Hyperion is another name for Helios the sun-god in Homer

14 **the nymph Calypso** the daughter of Atlas, the Titan (a son of Heaven and Earth) who supported the world. The word nymph indicates that she was a minor deity to be distinguished from the major deities who dwelt on Mount Olympus

18 **Ithaca** Odysseus's island home off north-west Greece. Its precise identification is a matter of dispute

20 **Poseidon** god of the sea, and brother of Zeus and Hades. One of his epithets is 'girdler of the earth' presumably from the Homeric belief that the , earth is surrounded by Ocean stream. He is also responsible for earthquakes and so is called the earthshaker. The emblem of his power is the trident, a three-pronged spear. One of the most powerful Olympians who hates Odysseus because he has blinded his son Polyphemus the Cyclops (see lines 68–71)

22 **Ethiopians** from the Homeric point of view, a remote people living at the edge of the world

27 **Olympian Zeus** the son of Cronos, whose rule he overthrew, and parent of many of the other gods. He is the most powerful of the Olympians, often referred to as their king, and his special province is the upper air where he controls storms and clouds and sends rain. His power is expressed in his thunderbolt (see Book 12, lines 405–17). He thunders to encourage Odysseus at Book 20, lines 102–19. Another of his emblems is the eagle.

There is a famous description of Olympus, a mountain in northern Greece and the home of the gods, at Book 6, lines 43–5

30 **Agamemnon** son of Atreus and brother of Menelaus, the husband of Helen. Leader of the Greek expeditions against Troy he was killed on his return by his wife Clytemnestra and her paramour Aegisthus

38 **Hermes** messenger of the gods. On the orders of Zeus (his father) he killed Argus, a monster with a hundred eyes, whom Hera (the wife of Zeus) had ordered to watch over Io, a beautiful young woman transformed into a cow by Zeus to cover up his amour with her

44 **Athene** virgin warrior goddess, daughter of Zeus and champion of Odysseus. Also goddess of wisdom

61 **Argives** literally natives of Argos which, in Homeric usage, often means simply the Greek mainland south of the isthmus of Corinth, so Argives are Greeks. Also known as Achaeans and Danaans

105 **Taphian** pirates and sea traders living north of Ithaca (see Book 19, lines 424–30)

113 **Telemachus** meaning far fighter. He gives Athene the welcome traditional for guests and strangers. The Greek for stranger is *zeinos*, whence zenophobia. A great ethical imperative in *The Odyssey* is zenophilia (the offering of hospitality to strangers)

154 **Phemius** meaning praiser, he who gives fame. Note that he is not willingly a party to the Suitors' behaviour

179 **'I will tell you everything honestly'** the first of many traveller's tales. She claims that her family and that of Telemachus are guest friends, that is, families who have exchanged hospitality and so have claims upon one another

241 **the Storm-Fiends have snatched him** Odysseus fearing death by drowning similarly laments that he could not have died heroically at Troy (see Book 5, lines 299–312)

246 **Dulichium, Same and Zacynthus** neighbouring islands. There are over 100 Suitors (see Book 16, lines 245–51)

276 **her father** Icarius, a Spartan and brother of Tyndareus, father of Helen. In Homeric times a wife could not inherit property in her own right. It seems here that the Suitors are required to give gifts to the bride's father

284 **Nestor** the oldest of the Greeks at Troy, famous for his advice and tactical skill. He is somewhat garrulous

286 **Menelaus** now reunited with Helen with whom he lives in tranquil amity. All
is forgiven (see Book 4)

297 **no longer a child** Telemachus's coming of age sets the plot in motion

311 **present ... one gives to a guest** a feature of Homeric hospitality (see Book
15, lines 80–5)

383 **Antinous** the name suggests one who is antagonistic. The Suitors, like
Penelope, are surprised at Telemachus's boldness

386 **heir to this island realm** this is not necessarily the head of Odysseus's
house. Telemachus claims merely his father's house and property as his
patrimony

437 **tunic** close-fitting shift made of linen which reached below the knees. A
large woollen cloak thrown over the shoulders was worn out of doors

BOOK 2   **The debate in the Ithacan assembly. Telemachus begins
his journey**

In the Ithacans' assembly Telemachus denounces the Suitors' behaviour.
Their leader Antinous in reply blames Penelope for delaying and not
making up her mind. He advises Telemachus to send his mother to
her father's house so that a new marriage can be arranged. An omen
is interpreted by a soothsayer as portending Odysseus's return and a
battle with the Suitors. Eurymachus angrily dismisses the soothsayer,
reiterating Antinous's advice to Telemachus. Telemachus then requests a
ship to make his journey to find definite news of his father. Athene
encourages Telemachus in his projected journey. Preparations are made
and he sets out at night.

> In the assembly the problem of Penelope's remarriage is debated.
> The facts of the situation necessary for the plot are clear. The *de
> facto* choice lies with Penelope, and the Suitors will press their suit
> until she chooses one of them. But Telemachus rebukes them for
> not having the courage to go directly to her father, so that he could
> make terms with the man of his choice (lines 50–4). They reply that
> it is up to Telemachus to send his mother back to her father's house
> himself (lines 133–4; 195–7). This for reasons financial and moral
> he is unwilling to do. The Suitors are allowed a point of view, and
> the problem of Penelope's remarriage is a complicated one that is
> not presented in black and white terms. Nevertheless, the omen

from Zeus following Telemachus's threat to Antinous confirms the judgment against the Suitors already given by Athene, and the soothsayer's interpretation functions as a warning of the consequences of their iniquitous behaviour. Leocritus's outburst (lines 242–51) to the effect that, even if Odysseus were to return, he would meet with a sticky end, further darkens their cause.

At the opening of the assembly, Telemachus's public rebuke to the Suitors ends in a burst of tears and general embarrassment, but he retrieves his dignity with his decision to go and search for news of his father, which shows courage and initiative that surprise the Suitors. Nevertheless, they have the upper hand. Mentor, to whom Odysseus had entrusted Telemachus, is powerless to help him and although the institution of the assembly might suggest some kind of wider forum, in fact there is no external authority to which Telemachus can appeal.

The stratagem of the web establishes that Penelope is not simply a figure of suffering, but a woman of intelligence and cunning, associated like her husband (line 116) with the goddess Athene.

7 **Assembly** held in the market place. The Greek word *agora* means market place, assembly and council. This is the ancestor of the assembly that was the cornerstone of the Athenian democracy. Here the assembly has no effective power

18 **Ilium** another name for Troy, from Ilus, according to some accounts the founder of the city

19 **the Cyclops** Odysseus tells his story in Book 9

38 **Peisenor** means man persuader, an appropriate name for a herald

40 **A crowd of Suitors** Telemachus argues that the people of Ithaca should feel outrage and shame at the Suitors' behaviour. (Most of them are from neighbouring islands.) Their conduct shows no sense of shame. The Greek word *aidos* means a restraining sense of shame, self-respect, honour

68 **Themis** the personification of the order of things established by law, custom and equity, so that she is described as the convener of assemblies here

81 **he burst into tears** showing his inexperience

116 **Athene** also presides over the mechanical arts such as spinning and weaving

120 **Tyro** beloved of Poseidon from whom Nestor and Jason the Argonaut were descended (see Book 11, line 235)

120 **Alcmene** beloved of Zeus by whom she bore Heracles (see Book 11, line 266)

120 **Mycene** a daughter of Inarchus, a river god of the Argive plain, who gave her name to Mycenae

135 **Avenging Furies** they avenge offences in the family; the Furies pursue Orestes after he has killed his mother Clytemnestra

146 **eagles** the birds of Zeus

157 **Halitherses Mastor's son** means sea-bold, son of seeker, appropriate for a fearless soothsayer

175 **in the twentieth year** ten years at Troy and nine years returning

225 **Mentor** his name has become proverbial for a guide or protector. He makes it clear that the Suitors are a small minority when compared with numbers at the Ithacan assembly

280 **So forget the Suitors** they have neither understanding nor a sense of what is right (*dike*)

310 **sagacious Telemachus replied** he was just a child when the Suitors first came; now that he has grown up things will be different

328 **Ephyre** Athene had told of Odysseus's journey to Ephyre in search of poison to smear on his arrows (Book 1, lines 257–64)

BOOK 3   Telemachus with Nestor at Pylos

Telemachus arrives at Pylos where he finds Nestor and his sons sacrificing to Poseidon on the shore. Nestor welcomes him, reminisces about Odysseus, tells of the fate of the returning Greeks and offers advice to Telemachus. He stays overnight with Nestor, and, after a morning sacrifice, sets off for Sparta to see Menelaus, accompanied by Nestor's son Peisistratus.

> At Pylos and Sparta the audience is reminded of the heroic past and the suffering of the Greeks at Troy, which is the backcloth to the present action and so the scope of the poem is widened. Nestor's account of the storm that divided the fleet returning home and of Agamemnon's death (in which Aegisthus bears the brunt of the blame) integrates Odysseus's fate with that of the other Greeks, and exposes the dangerous position of the war

heroes returning to the different insecurities of the post-war world. His exhortation to Telemachus to be as brave as Orestes, echoing Athene's earlier sentiments (Book 1, line 298), reinforces the poem's straightforward moral dimension.

After the disorder in Ithaca, here is Homeric civilisation at its best. Nestor and his sons show reverence to the gods and welcome the visiting strangers unconditionally. Athene disguised as Mentor specifically commends the good manners of Nestor's son in giving her as the elder the cup first (line 52). As always, the revelation of the immortal presence (line 372) comes as a surprise after the mortals have proved themselves worthy. Their sacrifice to the goddess that follows has all the appearance of a rite and ceremony scrupulously performed.

Nestor's reminiscences of Odysseus recall his pre-eminence among the Greeks as a strategist and his persuasiveness as an orator. His references to Athene's affection for Odysseus (in the presence of Athene in disguise) and his prediction that Odysseus will return (not believed by Telemachus) are powerfully **ironic**.

4 **Neleus** Nestor's father, who according to some accounts built the royal palace at Pylos

5 **sacrificing ... bulls** the thighs wrapped in fat and soaked in wine were offered to the gods. Bulls are associated with Poseidon elsewhere

36 **Peisistratus** means persuader of the army; doubtless he was so named from the persuasive powers of his father Nestor

42 **Who bears the aegis** the tasselled aegis, described *Iliad*, Book 5, lines 738ff, is some kind of defensive armour, probably a shield, the means of raising tempests and creating panic among mortals

52 **The goddess was delighted** she calls Peisistratus *dikaios*. Note how she had earlier dismissed the Suitors for lacking *dike* (a sense of what is right)

68 **Nestor, the Gerenian** so called because he had been among the Gerenians when Heracles invaded Pylos and killed all his brothers

91 **Amphitrite** a sea goddess; or simply the sea

107 **Priam** the old king of Troy, father of Hector and Paris

109 **Achilles** the strong man of the Greeks whose anger is the subject of the *Iliad*

109 **Ajax** a stout man in defence, second only to Achilles in fighting power. After the death of Achilles, killed by an arrow in his heel from Paris, there was a dispute as to who should receive his famous armour which had been made by the god Hephaestus. It was claimed by both Odysseus and Ajax, and went to Odysseus. Ajax planned a night attack on his own allies but Athene drove him mad, with the result that he killed a flock of sheep instead. When he came to his senses, he committed suicide in shame

110 **Patroclus** Achilles's comrade whose death in the sixteenth book is the pivotal action of the *Iliad*

112 **Antilochus** killed by Memnon, son of the dawn goddess Aurora. He takes part in the chariot race in the funeral games in honour of Patroclus

135 **the fatal anger ... Sire** one of the Greeks had raped Cassandra, the prophetic daughter of Priam in the temple of Athene. The Greeks failed to punish the offender so that Athene prevailed upon Poseidon to raise a storm which scattered the returning fleet

136 **the two sons of Atreus** Agamemnon and Menelaus

159 **Tenedos** an island off the Trojan coast

167 **Diomedes** another of the famous Greek fighters at Troy. In *Iliad* Book 5 he even wounds the gods

189 **Achilles' noble son** Pyrrhus, also called Neoptolemus. The Myrmidons are the followers of Achilles and Pyrrhus

190 **Philoctetes** the dying Heracles gave him his bow and arrows which were an indispensable part of Troy's downfall

191 **Idomeneus** his exploits feature in *Iliad* Book 8

196 **a son** Agamemnon's son Orestes; compare Athene's exhortation at Book 1, lines 298–302

278 **Sunium** on the south-east of Attica, of which region Athens is the capital

279 **Phoebus Apollo** the sun god; *phoebos* means bright. He is also an archer

287 **Malea** the most easterly of the three large promontories of the Peloponnese

326 **Lacedaemon** another name for Sparta

366 **the Cauconians** a tribe living not far from Pylos

378 **the august lady of Triton** many of Homer's **epithets** are of uncertain meaning

410 **Hades Halls** Hades was the brother of Zeus and Poseidon. He was king of the underworld in which resided the spirits of the dead

464 **Polycaste ... Telemachus** women regularly wash men in the Homeric poems

488 **Pherae** probably in Arcadia, halfway between Pylos and Sparta

BOOK 4   **Telemachus with Menelaus and Helen at Sparta. The Suitors plot to kill him as he returns**

Arriving at Sparta, Telemachus is welcomed by Menelaus and Helen who grieve over the past and tell of their memories of Odysseus, including the story of the Wooden Horse. On the following day Telemachus asks for news of his father. Menelaus tells of his own homecoming and how he met Proteus in Egypt who told him of the homecoming of other Greek leaders including Odysseus. Telemachus is prevailed upon to stay at Sparta. Back in Ithaca the Suitors plot to ambush him on his return. Penelope hears about it but is comforted in a dream sent by Athene.

> Domestic harmony prevails at Sparta, marked by the wedding celebrations with which the narrative begins. The material splendour of the setting is far from 'Spartan' in the later meaning of bare and ascetic. Menelaus's tearful regret for Odysseus, chief of his lost comrades, before he knows Telemachus's identity, has **pathetic** and **ironic** effect. The anodyne which Helen adds to the wine to take away the sting of painful memories effects a skilful transition to a gentler mood as she bids the company feast and take delight in story-telling (line 239). Her tale in which Odysseus adopts the disguise of a beggar to gather intelligence of the Trojans shows the kind of nerve and intelligence he will need later in Ithaca. His characterisation is confirmed and continued in Menelaus's story of his presence of mind in the Wooden Horse and of his physical prowess as a wrestler. The romantic and exotic tale of Menelaus's encounter with Proteus in Egypt anticipates the later adventures of Odysseus. Through Proteus we learn of the fate of other Greeks: Ajax and Agamemnon again and finally of Odysseus, kept prisoner on a desert island by the nymph Calypso.

> There is a marked contrast towards the end of the book with the behaviour of the Suitors in Ithaca. The plot to ambush and kill Telemachus puts them unambiguously in the wrong. The comforting dream sent to Penelope by Athene is only partial; it is a requirement of the plot that the protagonists be kept in the dark.

14 **golden Aphrodite** the goddess of love and beauty

83 **Cyprus ... Libya** Menelaus travelled from east to west throughout the Mediterranean, in seven years, amassing a fortune – though Homer does not say by what means

122 **Artemis** sister of Apollo, the beautiful goddess of chastity. Helen's wifely domestication is apparent in the emphasis on her spinning

131 **the basket ... on wheels** Mycenaean craftsmanship was highly sophisticated

220 **a drug** Egyptian medicine had been highly developed

232 **Pæeon** the word means healer in Greek

247 **Disguised as a beggar** prefiguring the later disguise

261 **suffered ... of heart** Helen repents: saying she was the victim of infatuation

276 **Deiphobus** after Hector was killed by Achilles, Deiphobus became leader of the Trojans, and after the death of Paris he married Helen

335 **just as if a deer** the first extended **simile** in the *Odyssey*

343 **Philomeleides** the name suggests a lover of limbs, that is, someone who cultivates physical fitness appropriate for a wrestler

365 **Eidothee** Menelaus' tale of her is a typically Odyssean adventure

499 **Ajax** not the Ajax who quarrelled with Odysseus but the son of Oileus. His boast shows him to be guilty of *hubris*, arrogant behaviour that offends the gods

513 **Hera** the wife (and sister) of Zeus and queen of heaven. She supported the Greek cause at Troy and is prominent in the *Iliad*. She has little to do in the *Odyssey*

517 **Thyestes** brother of Atreus, which means that Aegisthus and Agamemnon are cousins

563 **the Elysian Fields** the Homeric paradise

564 **Rhadamanthus** a son of Zeus and brother of King Minos of Crete. Because of his uprightness in life he was made a judge of the underworld after his death and took up his abode in Elysium

622 **Sidon** a rich city famous for craftsmen

BOOK 5   **Calypso is ordered by Zeus to release Odysseus. On his return he is cast ashore on the Isle of the Phaeacians**

Zeus sends Hermes to order Calypso to let Odysseus return home. She is reluctant, but tells Odysseus to make preparations, He builds a raft and sets sail. As he comes in sight of Scherie, Poseidon wrecks his boat in a storm. Only after great difficulty and peril does he reach land.

The repetition of the heavenly council, which may be regarded as a skilful means of returning to the main plot, the outcome of which is never in doubt, confirms the destiny of Odysseus and thus the doom of the Suitors. The wild beauty surrounding the cave of Calypso is to be contrasted with the cultivated beauty of the gardens of Alcinous in Phaeacia (Book 7, line 112). Homer makes it clear that Odysseus, wholly set on return, is constrained by Calypso; he draws a discreet veil over what is not to his purpose, the nature of the hero's relations with Calypso in the previous seven years.

Odysseus's habitual craft and caution are apparent in his dealings with the powerful goddess. He does not trust her and seeks to elicit an oath from her that she will not plot against him. His practical resourcefulness is apparent in the long account of his building of the raft. His heroic spirit is apparent when imagines that he is about to be drowned when Poseidon has shipwrecked him and he wishes he had perished honourably on the battlefield at Troy. On his first appearance he is both resourceful and long suffering.

1 **Tithonus** he fell in love with Dawn and prayed for immortality so that he could love her always. This the gods granted to him, but they did not give him immortal youth, so that he lived eternally in ever increasing decrepitude

50 **Pierian range** a mountainous district in Macedonia in northern Greece

55 **the remote island** of Calypso: named as Ogygia at Book 7, line 254

63 **The cave** a famous description

121 **Orion** a giant hunter who became a constellation

125 **Demeter** goddess of the earth

178 **Now let earth ...** the gods are not to be trusted unless they swear an oath. The most solemn oath is by Styx, the river of the underworld of death

199 **ambrosia** the word means immortal, and is used for the food eaten by the immortals

272 **Pleiads ... Bootes** the latter is the ploughman

the Great Bear is still visible in the sky after the other stars have set

283 **the Solymi** a people in or near Lycia in Asia Minor

299 **Poor wretch ...** Odysseus's lament shows his heroic spirit in wishing for a death that would have made him famous

333 **Ino** an insignificant minor deity only mentioned here

335 **Leucothoe** means white goddess

381 **Aegae** an island off Euboea

BOOK 6   **Odysseus meets Nausicaa**

Nausicaa, daughter of Alcinous, king of the Phaeacians, is prompted by Athene to go with her maids to wash clothes in a nearby river. Here Odysseus is awakened by their cries as they play a game with a ball. He approaches Nausicaa and asks for help which she willingly gives in the form of food, clothing and directions to the palace. She advises him to supplicate her mother Queen Arete. Odysseus travels to the palace after her to avoid scandal and reaches the city.

> After the storm, the encounter with Nausicaa represents a complete change of mood to tranquillity and joy. In his delicate concern for the young princess, Odysseus reveals a new aspect of his character, his tact in human relations and sense of fittingness. When Athene enhances his appearance (line 229), the **simile** that follows featuring the craftsman who provides an added sheen to his handiwork gives added expression to the Greek feeling for beauty in people and things. The episode is well integrated into the developing plot; Odysseus, a destitute stranger in a foreign land, needs to win the confidence of the Phaeacians, if he is to complete his journey home.

1 **the Phaeacians** Zeus refers to them as kinsmen of the gods (Book 6, line 35)

5 **the Cyclopes** individuals without the social bond; they are sharply contrasted with the Phaeacians

8 **Scherie** probably imaginary. Some have identified it with Corcyra (now Corfu)

12 **Alcinous** his name suggests strength of mind

102 **Artemis** goddess of chastity and also of hunting and is closely associated with the natural world

104 **Taygetus or Erymanthus** mountains in the Peloponnese

105 **the nymphs** in Greek myth there are indwelling spirits in all natural things

106 **Leto** mother of the twins Artemis and Apollo by Zeus

142 **throw his arms ... knees** a usual mode of supplication in Greek culture

162 **Delos** a small island in the Aegean on which Apollo and Artemis were born. A sacred place

233 **Hephaestus** god of metalwork; the divine artificer

BOOK 7   **Odysseus arrives at the palace of Alcinous**

The palace and gardens of Alcinous are described. Odysseus enters, and petitions Arete for help to return home. He is given food and drink, and promised the desired passage home. In answer to Arete's questioning he tells of his journey from Ogygia to Scherie.

> Phaeacia is represented almost as the Greek ideal. The palace is opulent and beautiful with artworks made by Hephaestus himself. The garden represents nature beautifully and productively ordered. The Phaeacians are skilled in seafaring, fabric making and the gentler arts of peace. They welcome the visiting stranger unconditionally and treat him with the utmost courtesy. Their civility towards Odysseus and amongst themselves is contrasted with the barbarity of their former neighbours, the Cyclopes, cave-dwellers who have no social bonds. Amongst them the blind bard, Demodocus (surely representative of the Homeric bard himself) has an honoured place. They enjoy too competing in games. In Phaeacia is an ideal blend of the physical and the artistic, the useful and the aesthetic.

> Scherie is an idealised and romantic island well suited to the chief function it has to serve as the setting for Odysseus's account of his fabulous adventures. It is cut off from the haunts of men (Book 6, line 8); the Phaeacians are kinsmen of the gods (Book 5, line 35) and have magic ships. It is a rich land whose inhabitants know only of war as a subject of song while they pursue the occupations of peace. It is Odysseus's last port of call in the world of romance before he returns to the realities of rugged Ithaca.

8 **Eurymedusa** means wide-ruling, a dignified name

55 **Arete** the name means she who is prayed for or to

58 **Eurymedon** Arete and Alcinous are of divine descent

80 **Marathon** on the coast of Attica, twenty-six miles from Athens

81 **Erechtheus** legendary king of Athens. The Erechtheum on the Acropolis is named after him

85–103 **the high-roofed halls ... employed** a magnificent building (compare the palace of Menelaus, Book 4, lines 43–51)

112–32 **Just outside ... house itself** the formal garden might be contrasted with the wildness of Calypso's cave

197 **Destiny and the relentless Fates** later writers distinguished three Fates: Clotho who spins the wool, Lachesis who measures and allots the thread, and Atropos who cuts it

321 **more remote than Euboea** this implies that Scherie is to the west of the Greek mainland

324 **Tityus** a giant who lived in Euboea. He attempted to rape Leto and was cast into Tartarus, the place of punishment in Hades, where a vulture devoured his liver. Nothing is known about the visit to him of Rhadamanthus (see Book 11, lines 576–81). The allusion, like the excursus on the ancestry of the king and queen, serves to enhance the Phaeacians by association with characters famous in old myth and legend

BOOK 8   The Phaeacian Games and the blind bard Demodocus

In the Phaeacian assembly it is agreed to send Odysseus home by ship. Alcinous proposes to entertain his guest and the Phaeacians. There is a banquet in the palace after which the blind bard Demodocus sings. Games follow. Odysseus is provoked into competing by the insult of a young Phaeacian. He distinguishes himself with the discus. Demodocus sings of the love of Ares and Aphrodite. Dancing follows. Odysseus receives gifts from his hosts. After supper Demodocus sings of the Wooden Horse. Odysseus's tearful response is noted by Alcinous who asks him to give an account of himself. (See Extended Commentaries, Text 1, for discussion of lines 487–547.)

There is **pathos** and **irony** when Demodocus in the presence of Odysseus, who has still not declared his identity, sings of the quarrel between Achilles and Odysseus at Troy and then later of the Wooden Horse. In the games, Odysseus proves his physical excellence. Alcinous lists Phaeacian accomplishments at line 247 as a prelude to the song that Demodocus sings about the adulterous love of Ares and Aphrodite. The lovers are ridiculed but the song vindicates the cleverness of Hephaestus the artificer and so accords with the values celebrated in the poem at large. Symbolically speaking, art triumphs over love and war. Odysseus's tears at the last song concerning the Wooden Horse are the frank expression of a nature that is sensitive to suffering.

44 **Demodocus** means esteemed by the people

73 **the famous deeds of heroes** Achilles consoles himself by singing of the deeds of famous men at *Iliad* Book 9, line 186

75 **the Quarrel of Odysseus and Achilles** not referred to elsewhere in Homer. Ancient commentators record that after the death of Hector the two quarrelled as to whether Troy could best be taken by force of arms or by a stratagem, Odysseus favouring the latter

79 **Apollo** also god of prophecy. His most famous oracle was at Delphi in northern Greece, formerly known as Pytho after the dragon (python) killed there by Apollo. Oracles were delivered through the medium of priests who were inspired by the god, and were sought by military and political leaders throughout the Greek world over many centuries

111 **Acroneos** means topship. All the names here have nautical associations, appropriate for a seafaring people

115 **Ares** god of war

147 **nothing makes a man ... feet** note the desire for excellence, characteristic of Homeric man in sport as in the more serious aspects of life

159 **Euryalus ... insulted him** the heroic spirit despises trade and the pursuit of material gain. Menelaus, however, spends seven years amassing treasure, and piracy seems to be almost an acceptable pastime in the *Odyssey*. There is perhaps some ambivalence here

167 **good looks, brains and eloquence** Odysseus does in fact have all these desirable qualities (note the famous description of him at Book 6, lines 229–35). In this respect he represents the Greek ideal

219 **Philoctetes** to whom Heracles gave his bow and arrows. Doubtless much is made of Odysseus's skill in archery here because of the role it will play in the final dénouement

224 **Heracles ... or Eurytus** the former is a son of Zeus, famous for his twelve labours. The latter, according to some accounts, was Heracles's teacher in the art of bowmanship. Both were heroes of a previous generation

248 **But the things ... beds** as a result of these lines the Phaeacians have been regarded as overfond of soft and luxurious living. Yet they also boast of their prowess in sport and they are expert seamen. As for hot baths, Odysseus himself takes pleasure in one after the games (Book 8, lines 450–2). In the life of the Phaeacians there is a blend of the practical and the athletic with the aesthetic which is characteristically Greek

258–61 **nine official stewards ... performance** the preparation of the hall is a further indication of the well-ordered society

266 **the love of Ares and Aphrodite** a famous comic interlude which has been much censured on the grounds of its immorality, though it could be argued that it is highly moral, since adultery is made ridiculous and punished. The tale shows the triumph of craft and intelligence over passion and strength

283 **Lemnos** the island on which Hephaestus fell when he was thrown from heaven (see *Iliad* Book 1, lines 590–4)

285 **Ares of the golden reins** Ares is frequently represented as riding furiously in his war chariot

294 **Sintian friends** the inhabitants of Lemnos who rescued Hephaestus after he had been flung from heaven

306 **Father Zeus** Zeus is father of both Ares and Aphrodite and, according to some accounts, of Hephaestus too

353 **wriggle out of his debt** a fine for adultery: even a homicide could be expiated by money

361 **Thrace** a wild region east of Macedonia always associated with Ares

364 **the Graces** usually thought to be three in number

488 **Apollo** the god not only of prophecy but also of poetry

500 **took it up at the point where** implies that the whole Trojan saga is now part of the bard's repertoire

522 **wet with the tears** Homeric heroes have no inhibition about displays of grief (compare Achilles at *Iliad* Book 1, lines 348–63 and elsewhere)

565 **Poseidon grudged us** he is a morose and malevolent deity in the *Odyssey*. He is the only god not to laugh at Ares and Aphrodite (line 344)

BOOK 9   **Odysseus begins recounting his adventures with his encounter with the Lotus-eaters and the Cyclops**

Odysseus reveals his identity and begins the narrative of his wanderings after the fall of Troy with an account of the sack of Ismarus and his encounter with the Cicones. He and his men are blown from Cape Malea to north Africa where they encounter the Lotus-eaters. They sail to Sicily where they are imprisoned by the Cyclops in his cave. Odysseus makes the Cyclops drunk, blinds him and then escapes, clinging to the underside of the Cyclops's sheep as they are let out of the cave in the morning.

Not only does Odysseus give voice at the opening to the Greek idealism that pervades the poem, but perhaps, because he is at a court where the domestic virtues (concentrated in Arete) are celebrated, he also utters the simple truth that there is no place like home. The prospect of divinity offered by Calypso and the life of pleasure offered by Circe never won his heart; rugged Ithaca is sweeter to his imagination than dwelling in a rich house in a foreign land (line 36).

After these gentle sentiments, the first incident in the tale he tells, his sacking of the city of the Cicones, comes as a shock. This is a realistic tale of piracy, like other tales told in the Ithacan narrative in the second half of the poem, and so differs markedly from the rest of his after-dinner narrative told to Alcinous, though the folly shown by his followers anticipates their later folly in eating the oxen of the Sun, which causes their destruction. The piratical theme is continued in the encounter with the Cyclops, when his men's first instinct is to plunder his produce (line 224). Although the Cyclops is monstrous in form and behaviour, his affection for his animals redeems him a little; it is a typical feature of Homeric narrative that, despite the clear moral outline, characters and incidents are seldom presented in black and white terms. Although the tales are designed to cast Odysseus in an heroic light and to illustrate his intelligence and craft, he is no more perfectly good than the Cyclops is perfectly bad. His reckless and vainglorious boast (line 475ff.) nearly cost him his life and those of his companions.

The narrative of his tales is necessary to account for his long absence. In the episode of the Lotus-eaters which threatens to extinguish the desire to return home, and the encounter with the Cyclops which accounts for the hostility of Poseidon, there are links to the main plot.

5 **myself feel ... perfection** this praise of the bard is a vivid evocation of a Homeric ideal (compare Book 17, lines 518–20)

19ff **I am Odysseus ...** pride in achievement and fame is characteristic of the Homeric heroes

32 **Aeaean** Aeaea is the island home of Circe

40 **Ismarus** in Thrace, north-east of Troy. The Cicones were allies of the Trojans

80 **Malea** the most easterly of the three promontories of the Peloponnese. Odysseus, therefore, was well on his way home when he was blown off-course

91 **the Lotus-eaters** located on the north African coast, so that it is to be inferred that Odysseus is blown right across the Mediterranean, due south of Greece, by the north wind

117 **the Cyclopes' country** identified as Sicily. Cyclops means round-eyed. The Cyclopes are said to be *athemistes* (having no regard for *themis*, custom, law or equity). They do not practise agriculture, and live each a law unto himself. This primitive state of nature is in marked contrast to the civilised life of the Phaeacians, once their neighbours before a previous king had removed them and settled them in Scherie (see Book 6, lines 4ff.). Odysseus's description of their island's unrealised potential serves to emphasise the achievement of the Phaeacians, and further suggests that Scherie is a desirable ideal, fully approved of by Homer

252 **'And who are you?'** Polyphemus's opening questions are a repetition of Nestor's questions at Book 3, lines 71–4. In view of Odysseus's treatment of the Cicones, suspicion of the stranger is natural and justified. Nestor's questions, however, were put after he had fed his guests

270 **Zeus ... champion of suppliants and guests** the laws of hospitality are a fundamental feature of Homeric society, and as central to the *Odyssey* as are the laws relating to treatment of the dead in the *Iliad*

366 **Nobody** a reminder that this tale is a very old one. Many versions of it exist in many cultures

475 **Cyclops! ...** contrast Odysseus's boasts with Book 22, lines 411–18 where Odysseus rebukes Eurycleia for boasting over the death of the Suitors. Odysseus's triumph is of wit and intelligence over brute strength (compare the triumph of Hephaestus over Ares)

BOOK 10   Odysseus's reminiscing continues: his meeting with
cannibal giants and Circe

Odysseus and his companions sail on to Aeolia where Aeolus gives
Odysseus a bag in which all the winds are imprisoned except the
favourable west wind. His companions undo the bag with disastrous
consequences. They come next to the land of the Laestrygonians, a race
of cannibalistic giants. They escape to Aeaea where Circe turns
Odysseus's men into swine. With the help of Hermes he masters
Circe who then ceases to be hostile. He spends a year with the goddess.
Before his departure Circe tells him that he must consult the spirit of
the prophet Teiresias in Hades.

> In the course of his tales Odysseus has to account for the loss
> of his companions. We have already been told in the opening lines
> of the poem that they died through their own witlessness and
> folly. In the encounter with Aeolus, it is his companions who
> foolishly open the bag containing the winds while Odysseus is
> asleep. Later when some of his companions have been turned
> into swine by Circe, Eurylochus advises him to cut their losses and
> flee; Odysseus says he feels compelled to go to their rescue. The
> duties of leadership and ties of obligation are clear. When he
> escapes from Circe's clutches for the first time (through the
> magic plant, moly, given to him by Hermes, a rare instance of a
> resort to magic in the main narrative), Odysseus nevertheless
> follows her instruction to come back to him together with his men.
> A lesser man might have made good his escape, not so the heroic
> Odysseus.
>
> We are allowed another perspective upon this adventurousness
> when Eurylochus warns his companions not to accompany
> Odysseus and puts the loss of their comrades in the Cyclops's
> cave directly down to his reckless folly. It is a measure of the
> many-sidedness of the poem that Odysseus's leadership can be
> questioned.
>
> Circe's instruction that he must visit the prophet Teiresias in Hades
> is not only dramatic in itself but a means of propelling the plot
> forward and linking the tales.

1 **Aeolia** north-west of Sicily, identified by some with the Lipari islands

2 **Aeolus** means changeful, an appropriate name for the ruler of the winds

199 **Antiphates** his name suggests contradiction

207 **Eurylochus** the only one of Odysseus's companions who is individualised

278 **Hermes ... looking like a young man** this is how he is always represented in Greek culture

305 **moly** probably imaginary. Circe's magic can be defeated only by magical means

429 **'Where are ... now?'** Eurylochus's rebuke is not without justice

491 **Persephone** daughter of Demeter and wife of Hades; queen of the underworld

492 **Teiresias** the most famous Greek prophet of a previous age

509 **the River of Ocean** Ocean is imagined as a stream encircling the earth (which is flat). It seems here that a descent into Hades is not envisaged. Odysseus must simply cross the Ocean stream. Elsewhere in Homer, however, Hades does seem to be located underground

528 **Erebus** means darkness

BOOK **11**   *Odysseus's narrative continued: his visit to Hades*

Following Circe's instructions, Odysseus summons up the spirits of the dead. He speaks first to Teiresias who warns him to avoid harming the oxen of the Sun, tells him of trouble at home, and prophesies his future. He then speaks with his mother Anticleia, who tells him about his father Laertes and about Penelope. There follows the catalogue of famous women. After this he pauses in his narration. Arete recommends that he be given more gifts. Alcinous enquires whether he saw any of his heroic comrades from the Trojan campaign. Odysseus then tells of his meeting with Agamemnon, Achilles and Ajax, and his sighting of other famous heroes.

Teiresias's prophecy serves the same function in the design of the poem that is served by the councils of the gods. It clarifies the plot as well as suggesting an inevitability about its destined end. The meeting with his mother and her account of his father's plight further humanises the hero, who is for a moment simply a mother's son. At the beginning of his narrative he had talked feelingly of home and parents and here he is seen in a new and tender light as he vainly tries to embrace his mother's spirit.

In the interlude, the Phaeacians are so spellbound by his account (Alcinous commends his skill with words, saying he has told his story with the skill of a bard [line 369]) that they decide to honour him with gifts. The hero thus acquires maximum status and honour in the eyes of both his fictional and his actual audience before his fateful journey home. He had arrived as a destitute beggar he will departs with his heroic status fully proved and recognised.

His various conversations with Agamemnon, Achilles and Ajax, his former comrades now dead, have great **pathos** and provide dramatic contrasts in character and fate. Agamemnon brings out the contrast between Clytemnestra and Penelope, whose faithfulness is a cornerstone of the plot.

The awesome character of Hades is emphasised in the accounts of the punishments of Tityus, Tantalus and Sisyphus. Finally the conversation with Heracles associates Odysseus with exceptional heroism and exceptional labours.

14 **Cimmerians** possibly meaning dwellers in darkness

51 **Elpenor** there is an apparent inconsistency here. Odysseus asks him how he died, having already given the circumstances of his death in the previous book. Elpenor asks to be cremated, the usual way of disposing of the dead in Homer

85 **Anticleia** Odysseus had been told by Circe not to speak to anyone before Teiresias

Autolycus a son of Hermes and Odysseus's grandfather, renowned for his cunning and for thieving (see Book 19, lines 394–6)

107 **Thrinacie** see Book 12, line 260 for the beginning of this episode

117 **insolent men** Teiresias's prophecy is given three years after Odysseus left Troy, and the Suitors did not begin to woo Penelope until later. This anachronism has been used in the argument against Homeric authorship of Book 11

121–36 **Take a well-cut ... prosperous people** nowhere else in Homer is Odysseus's future foretold. It implies further travels

129 **winnowing fan** a long pole with a shovel-shaped end with which the corn was thrown up against the wind to clear it of chaff. It resembled an oar in appearance

173 **Artemis ... gentle darts** evidently a formula for expressing a peaceful death

175 **Is my kingdom safe** as king of Ithaca Odysseus was accorded special rights in terms of land and entertainment. He was not the sole Ithacan chieftain (see Book 8, line 46 where sceptred nobles, twelve in number, attend Alcinous in council)

206–9 **Three times ... pain** when Odysseus is unable to embrace Anticleia, she explains the Homeric conception of the after-life

225 **all the women** all figures of a previous generation famous in heroic legend

235 **Tyro** she was illustrious in her descendants. Her son Neleus was the father of Nestor. Aeson was the father of Jason who led the Argonauts in quest of the Golden Fleece

240 **Enipeus** a river in Thessaly in northern Greece

256 **Iolcus** also in Thessaly, the town from which Jason sailed in his ship the Argo on his quest for the Golden Fleece

260 **Asopus** a river flowing through Boeotia

271 **Epicaste** called Jocasta by later writers. Homer does not mention the self-blinding of Oedipus

284 **Orchomenus** in Boeotia

291 **the gifted seer, Melampus** ancestor of Theoclymenus, whose history is given at Book 15, line 224

296 **Iphiclus** one of the Argonauts

298 **Leda** she was visited by Zeus in the form of a swan. The product of this union was Helen. Leda was also the mother of Clytemnestra by Tyndareus

300 **Polydeuces** more familiar in his Roman name of Pollux

315 **Ossa ... Pelion** mountains in Thessaly. To pile Pelion on Ossa became proverbial

318 **the son whom Leto ... bore** Apollo

321 **Phaedra** the daughter of Minos, wife of Theseus of Athens and stepmother of Hippolytus with whom she fell in love

Procris daughter of Erechtheus king of Athens, an unfaithful wife

Ariadne she helped Theseus, whom she loved, to find his way in the Labyrinth by means of a thread, thus saving him from the Minotaur, a monster with a bull's head. She was subsequently deserted by Theseus

Book 11 continued

325 **Dionysus** the god of wine, seldom mentioned in Homer

326 **Maera** a nymph who devoted herself to Artemis, who killed her when she broke her vow of chastity

326 **Eriphyle** when bribed with a gold necklace by Polyneices, Oedipus's son, she persuaded her husband Amphiarous to join the expedition of the Seven Against Thebes on which he was doomed to die

357 **loaded me with ... gifts** gifts bring honour and esteem. He approves of Penelope's attempt to extract gifts from the Suitors at Book 18, lines 281–3

422 **Cassandra** allotted to Agamemnon as a spoil of war

489-91 **I would rather ... dead** this is particularly poignant coming from Achilles, as he had been given a choice of a long life without distinction or a short one with achievement and fame. He chose the latter (*Iliad* Book 9, lines 410–16)

496 **Phthie** Achilles's home town in Thessaly. Peleus's fate here reminds us of Laertes, in the same way that mention of Clytemnestra brought Penelope to mind

509 **Scyros** according to later accounts, Achilles's mother Thetis had disguised him as a girl and introduced him to the daughters of Lycomedes of Scyros (an island in the Aegean) under the name of Pyrrha, so that he would not fight in the Trojan War. However, one of his companions bore Pyrrhus by him, thus uncovering his identity

539 **asphodel** a lean spiky plant

563-7 **He made no reply ... my heart** a famous moment, described as an example of sublimity in the treatise of the rhetorician Longinus (first century AD): *On the Sublime* IX, 2. Ajax had quarrelled with Odysseus over the weapons of Achilles (see Book 8)

568 **Minos** king of Crete in life and a judge in the underworld

572 **Orion** an active figure in contrast to those described previously. For this reason this passage is suspected to be a later interpolation. It has been thought strange that Odysseus can view scenes within the underworld. Prior to this the spirits have been coming to him

576 **Tityus** accorded in Greek myth, has the same punishment as Prometheus (the god who brought fire to mankind)

582 **Tantalus** according to some accounts he divulged the secrets of Zeus. In other accounts he abused the hospitality of the gods, hence his punishment. The word tantalise is derived from his fate

593 **Sisyphus** legend is not so clear about the original crime as it is about his subsequent punishment

601 **Heracles** he was immortalised by the gods

603 **Hebe** usually a cupbearer for the gods. Her name suggests the bloom of youth

617–26 **Heaven-born ... Hades' realm** the master of Heracles was Eurystheus for whom he was forced to carry out his twelve labours because of Hera's jealousy – he was a son of Zeus but not by her. One of his labours was the task of capturing Cerberus, a monstrous three-headed dog who guarded the gates of Hades

631 **Theseus and Peirithous** famous in legend for their friendship

634 **the gorgon head** in later accounts, the Gorgons had snakes writhing in their hair and faces which could turn men to stone

BOOK **12** **Odysseus continues his narrative: the Sirens, Scylla and Charybdis, the oxen of the Sun**

Circe, to whom he has returned, tells him of dangers to come. So that he can hear the song of the Sirens, he instructs his men to bind him to the mast while sealing their own ears with wax. He sails between Scylla and Charybdis; Scylla seizes six of his men. They come to Thrinacie where they are marooned for a month by unfavourable winds. When food has run out, his men, against his instructions, kill the oxen of the Sun while Odysseus is asleep. Zeus wrecks the fleet with a thunderbolt. Odysseus alone survives and drifts to the island of Ogygia.

> To absolve his hero of any blame for the loss of his companions, Homer makes Odysseus try to avoid landing on Thrinacie at all and makes Eurylochus, who had earlier questioned the wisdom of Odysseus's leadership, lead a rebellion against him. Even when forced to change his plan, Odysseus requires his men to swear an oath that they will do not kill any cattle or sheep that they find on the island. The groaning of the meat on the spits (line 395) is one of a number of supernatural events (e.g. Theoclymenus's vision [Book 20, line 351]) and the light in the hall (Book 19, line 34), of a kind not found in the *Iliad*, which serve to suggest an underlying fate.

39 **the Sirens** two in number

70 **the celebrated Argo** the ship in which Jason sailed with the Argonauts (those who sailed in the Argo). Jason belonged to the previous generation of heroes **Aeetes** Circe's brother who ruled in Colchis in the Black Sea

104 **Charybdis** the name suggests wide-swallower. The ancients thought that these two monsters were to be located in the straits of Messina between Italy and Sicily

127 **Thrinacie** a legendary island. This is Odysseus's second warning. Teiresias gave the first

132 **Phaethusa and Lampetie** their names suggest brightness

154 **the prophecies** Odysseus tells his crew of the prophecies, but does not tell them about Scylla, and he is not as clear as he could have been about the danger on Thrinacie

184 **the Sirens' song** irresistibly offers Odysseus knowledge

227 **I put my famous armour ... spears** Odysseus ignores Circe's advice. Homer preserves his independence in spite of the inevitability imparted by the use of prophecy

278 **Eurylochus** again the troublemaker. He had been critical of Odysseus before at Book 10, lines 431–7

BOOK 13   Odysseus is brought on a Phaeacian ship to Ithaca, where Athene meets him

The Phaeacians convey Odysseus to Ithaca by night and deposit him on the shore, asleep. In the morning he wakes up and does not recognise the place. Athene appears in the guise of a young shepherd, and Odysseus asks her where he is. She enlightens him. In response to her questions he tells his first Cretan tale to conceal his identity, saying he is on the run having killed a man. Athene is amused and reveals herself. They hide the treasure. Athene disguises Odysseus as an old beggar and sets him on the road to the hut of his loyal steward Eumaeus.

The arrival in Ithaca is replete with **irony**, when Odysseus fails to recognise the place and thinks the Phaeacians have broken their promise. They, meanwhile, are punished by Poseidon for their pains in being hospitable to Odysseus. His habitual craft is revealed when he invents a false identity for himself in conversation with Athene disguised as a shepherd. His tale that he is on the run as a result of a homicide is unromantic and realistic, fitting the change in the scene and his circumstances.

Athene's appreciative response establishes the affinity between them (line 296ff.). Her further appreciation of him at line 332 as 'so persuasive, so quick-witted, so self-possessed' highlights the intellectual and moral qualities that will be tested in the rest of the poem as he struggles to regain the mastery of his own house.

The conversation between them further explains why Athene has not appeared to him since the fall of Troy; she has been reluctant to oppose Poseidon whose malevolence has just been proved in his treatment of the Phaeacians. Athene also accounts for her failure to tell Telemachus the truth. Motivations necessary for the complex plot of the poem are made manifest at this pivotal point in the action.

The physical disguise, necessary for survival, is Athene's idea but Odysseus has already disguised his identity from her and so has proved himself worthy of the goddess's attention and attuned to the plan she suggests.

59 **My Queen ...** Odysseus's last words, as his first words, are addressed to Arete, she who is prayed to or for

96 **Phorycs** a minor sea deity

103 **cavern sacred to the Nymphs** a strange description that has attracted bizarre interpretation. The cave was thought to be an **allegory** of the world by Porphyrius of Tyre, a writer of the third century AD

104 **Naiads** usually fresh water spirits. (Dryads inhabit trees, Oreads mountains and Nereids the sea)

119 **still fast asleep** Homer has been much criticised for what has been regarded as an absurdity here. It is necessary for the plot that Odysseus lands unheralded and unheeded in his own country

128 **Father Zeus ...** Poseidon feels that he has been dishonoured. Zeus placates him. Both gods are somewhat malevolent here

217 **he checked his fine tripods** Odysseus's concern for his treasure reveals the Homeric heroes' due regard for the material things of this world, whether it be feasting and drinking, of which there is much in the *Odyssey*, or amassing treasure of which there are also many tales

242 **it is rugged** compare Athene's description of Ithaca with that of Telemachus at Book 4, lines 600–8

256 **in the spacious land of Crete** the first of several Cretan tales told by Odysseus. The Cretans, besides being great traders and adventurers, were also proverbial liars

260 **Orsilochus** means ambush-causer

285 **Sidon** in Phoenicia, now the Lebanon

408 **Arethusa** a Nereid, a sea nymph. Nereus was a god of the sea

BOOK 14   Odysseus (in disguise) visits his steward Eumaeus

Eumaeus welcomes the stranger at his door, feeds him, complains about the Suitors, and asks Odysseus about himself. His master in reply tells his second Cretan tale, saying he had heard of Odysseus in Thesprotia. Eumaeus does not believe this, but continues to treat him well. Odysseus tells a second tale of a night ambush at Troy in order to elicit a cloak and tunic from Eumaeus.

> The disguise enables Odysseus to see for himself that his steward is loyal. The testimony of Eumaeus proves Odysseus to be the good master. In welcoming the stranger unconditionally, Eumaeus fulfils the highest obligations of Homeric society. Homer quickly establishes his character and a key moral issue in the second half of the poem. He is associated with *themis* (line 56) custom and *dike* (line 84) right conduct. His condemnation of the Suitors' profligacy and the irregularity of their wooing has great moral force.

> There is a piquant **irony** in his refusal to believe the stranger's oath that Odysseus will return but in his acceptance of the false tale he is told (except for the details about Odysseus) and further irony in the stranger's assertion that he hates the man 'who is driven by poverty to lie' (line 156) as he is about to tell his false tale.

> In his second Cretan tale (line 192) Odysseus represents himself as an adventurer, entrepreneur and money-maker (compare Menelaus in Book 4). He had shown a great regard for the material gifts at Phaeacia and his tale shows this materialism in a more realistic mode. The stranger regards the Trojan War as little more than one

of a number of raiding expeditions which might be a source of potential wealth and good fortune.

When Eumaeus in return tells of the Aetolian stranger (line 379), Odysseus and the audience learn that the Ithacans have been regaled by tales of their master's return before, so that realistic grounds are laid for caution and disbelief not only in Eumaeus but also later in Telemachus and Penelope. In rebuking the stranger for telling him (as he believes) what he wants to hear, Eumaeus reveals his absolute moral worth. He is treating the stranger well not for any ulterior reason but out of uncontaminated respect for the laws of hospitality.

When the stranger makes a further test of Eumaeus (line 459) in telling the tale in which Odysseus uses his wits to procure a cloak for himself on a frosty night, Eumaeus enjoys the tale and good-humouredly gives him a cloak. There is cunning in the crafty way in which the stranger recounts the craft of Odysseus. Homer's Odyssean wit is here humorously revealed.

96 **enormously rich** Odysseus owns land on the mainland too

182 **Arceisius** Odysseus's paternal grandfather, a son of Zeus

315 **Thesprotia** to the north of Ithaca on the Greek mainland

316 **Pheidon** the name means he who spares

327 **Dodona** in Epirus, the site of the oldest and most famous oracle of Zeus, always associated with the oak trees that grew there

371 **Storm-Fiends ... away** compare the lament of Telemachus (Book 1, lines 234–40) and of Odysseus himself (Book 5, lines 299–312)

379 **Aetolia** a district in the south-west of the Greek mainland north of the Peloponnese

435 **Maia** a daughter of Atlas who gave birth to Hermes, a child of Zeus, on Mount Cyllene in Arcadia. Hermes was the god of herdsmen

455 **Mesaulius** the name means yardman. Eumaeus has his own servants showing that he is a figure of authority in Odysseus's household

452 **Taphians** a neighbouring people who traded by sea. Athene disguises herself as a Taphian sailor in Book 1, and Penelope reminds Antinous that Odysseus had saved his father from Taphian pirates (Book 16, lines 424–30)

510 **You shan't go without clothing** Eumaeus gives Odysseus clothing, but he is no fool, and has seen through Odysseus's motives in telling the tale

book 15　Telemachus returns to Ithaca and visits Eumaeus

Telemachus makes preparations to return to Ithaca from his expedition to Pylos and Sparta. He gives passage to Theoclymenus, who tells him he has killed a man and is on the run. Eumaeus tells Odysseus about his father Laertes and relates his own history. Telemachus returns.

The two strands of the plot are now joined with the return of Telemachus from Sparta. The courteous treatment of him by Menelaus on his departure again displays Homeric manners at their best.

The histories relating to Theoclymenus (lines 223–56) who is of noble family but who has fallen on hard times and Eumaeus (lines 381–484) also of noble origins but who is the victim of piracy are similar to the invented tales of the disguised Odysseus and evoke a world not of heroic values but one dominated by the vagaries of fortune and by human greed. This is the backdrop to the reestablishment of order in Ithaca.

68–85 **'Telemachus ... golden cup'** Menelaus's speech to Telemachus is famous for its typically Greek emphasis on moderation in all things (nothing in excess) and also for its proverbial line about the welcoming of the coming guest and the speeding of the departing guest

103 **Megapenthes** the name means great grief. He is the son of Menelaus by a slave girl (Helen could not bear him a son, but has a daughter, Hermione by him – see Book 4, lines 10–14)

160 **a bird ... the right** the right side is auspicious in Greek folklore

186 **Pherae** halfway between Sparta and Pylos. They return by the way they came

225 **Melampus** see also Book 11, lines 281–97. The relevance and point of this long history about him have often been questioned

247 **a woman's avarice** Eriphyle mentioned at Book 11, line 326

256 **Theoclymenus** the name means god-famed. It seems to be the regular Homeric practice that retribution for a homicide was a matter for the immediate kinsmen of the slain. In the *Iliad* Ajax remarks that gifts can expiate a homicide, so that compensation might settle the issue on occasion (Book 9, lines 632–7)

295 **Chalcis** a river south of the Alpheus in Elis. The place names mentioned here have been located on the coast south of Ithaca

363 **Ctimene** Odysseus's sister, only mentioned here. Her husband gave gifts for her as Eurymachus hopes to do for Penelope (Book 15, lines 17–18)

367 **Same** a neighbouring island

399 **the satisfaction of sharing … unhappy memories** a famous sentiment

403 **Syrie** identified with Delos

BOOK 16   Eumaeus tells Penelope that Telemachus has returned safely. Odysseus meets his son, who recognises him

Telemachus arrives at Eumaeus's hut where he meets the stranger whom he tells of the situation in the palace. He asks Eumaeus to go to the palace to tell Penelope that he has returned safely. Odysseus then reveals himself to his son. Together they plot the Suitors' destruction. When the Suitors hear that Telemachus has eluded their ambush, they discuss Antinous's suggestion that he be waylaid before he reaches the palace. Penelope, informed by Medon, hears of this discussion and roundly rebukes them. Eurymachus makes a soothing speech. Eumaeus returns to his hut and reports to Telemachus.

begg-

Telemachus's courtesy to the stranger is further proof of his decency and good manners. Through the disguise Odysseus learns first hand about the situation in his house, sees the difficulty of the situation from Telemachus's point of view and learns that his son genuinely desires his father's return.

After the emotional recognition scene, Telemachus sees the need for speed and is unwilling that Eumaeus go to the country to tell Laertes of his return, directing that one of Penelope's maids be sent instead. He offers good advice in conversation with Odysseus in the plan to kill the Suitors, modifying the plan to test the loyalty of the servants on the farms (line 311).

The plot advances to a critical phase when news of Telemachus's return reaches the palace. The Suitors fear that he will call an assembly to turn the people against them by exposing their plot against his life. Antinous, in a venomous speech, reveals his full iniquity. Even Eurymachus, the politic Suitor, who assures Penelope that Telemachus will be safe (line 448) is secretly plotting his destruction. Antinous's proposal that they divide the wealth of Odysseus between them (line 384) shows a realistic incentive for everyone; there will be something for everybody, not just for the lucky man chosen by Penelope.

17 **like a fond father welcoming back his son** a highly apposite **simile**

252 **Medon** the name means protector. One of the few noblemen loyal to Odysseus, he informs Penelope of the plot against her son

376–93 **Mark my words ... husband** Antinous fears public opinion: for the first time the Suitors are on the defensive, having been outwitted by Telemachus

394 **Amphinomus** the most intelligent and sympathetic of the Suitors. His advice shows political shrewdness

BOOK 17 **Telemachus returns to the palace, with Odysseus and Eumaeus following: their encounters with the goatherd and Odysseus's old dog**

Truth

Telemachus goes to the palace and is welcomed by Eumaeus and Penelope. The prophet Theoclymenus declares that Odysseus has already returned home. Telemachus tells Penelope of his journey. Odysseus sets out for the palace and is insulted by the goatherd Melanthius. Odysseus is recognised by his old dog Argus. He enters the palace and proceeds to beg from the Suitors. Antinous in anger throws a stool at him. Eumaeus tells Penelope that the stranger claims to have seen Odysseus. Penelope asks to see him.

The disguised Odysseus suffers indignities from the goatherd Melanthius (a foil to Eumaeus) on the way to the palace and from Antinous when he arrives. In the first instance his self-control is tested and in the palace he experiences for himself the Suitors' profligacy. Their condemnation of Antinous shows at least some respect for traditional manners. The condition of Odysseus's old dog Argus, flee-ridden and neglected on a dunghill outside the palace, has strong **symbolic** force. The air of indignity is further intensified by the realistic way in which Odysseus acts the part of the beggar, with much talk of the urgent needs of his ravening belly.

The dramatic confrontation with Antinous in which he repeats a shortened version of his Cretan tale allows Odysseus to confront the Suitors' leader with unwelcome truths, that he is too mean-spirited even to give scraps of bread from another man's table. The indignities he suffers further alienate the audience from the Suitors raising indignation on his behalf.

46 **'do not bring me to tears'** Telemachus rebukes Penelope: for the second time (compare Book 1, lines 346–61). Again Penelope is taken aback

68 **Halitherses** the soothsayer who had prophesied the Suitors' doom in the first Ithacan assembly

101 **'Telemachus, I am going upstairs'** throughout the poem there is some tension between son and mother

172 **Medon** he has a foot in both camps

207 **Ithacus** it is to be presumed that he gave his name to Ithaca, just as Neritus gave his name to the mountain

212 **Melanthius** the one manservant of Odysseus who proved disloyal; a foil to Eumaeus

292 **Argus** the name means swift. The ship Argo is appropriately named. Argus's neglect has **symbolic** force, though the details are fully natural

375 **'How typical ...'** a fine sarcasm in Antinous's speech here to Eumaeus

396 **I appreciate your fatherly concern** Telemachus returns the sarcasm to Antinous

491 **I hope the Archer ...** Penelope's exclamation introduces the motif of the bow

541 **a loud sneeze** an omen

BOOK 18   **Disguised as a beggar, Odysseus fights Irus. Penelope accepts gifts from the Suitors**

The Suitors entertain themselves by provoking a sparring match between the stranger and the beggar Irus. (See Extended Commentaries, Text 2 for discussion of lines 66–117.) Odysseus warns Amphinomus of the retribution awaiting the Suitors. Penelope appears before the Suitors to elicit gifts from them. Odysseus is insulted by a maidservant Melantho, and mocked by Eurymachus who throws a stool at him. Telemachus intervenes to bring peace to the palace.

The further indignities inflicted upon the disguised Odysseus meet with Athene's approval as she 'wished the anguish to bite deeper yet into the heart of Odysseus' (line 347). Homer uses the goddess here to clarify his own design in the plot. The beggar's **homily** on the insecurity of the human condition (line 130ff.) enunciates one of the moral themes of the poem but also advances the plot, for it serves as a warning of the imminent change of fortune and of the judgement to come. Amphinomus's recognition of its justice is an admission of the Suitors' guilt which further vindicates Odysseus in the punishment he plans for them. His recognition that Amphinomus is comparatively blameless and his wish that he return home before the day of reckoning shows a moral discrimination in the hero that is ignored by the goddess who has determined that it is Amphinomus's fate to die with the rest (line 155). Homer has used the **divine machinery** here to absolve his hero of blame for the apparently indiscriminate slaughter at the end.

A key element in the plot is clarified with Penelope's account of Odysseus's instructions to her when he left for Troy. She was to wait for him till Telemachus became a bearded man then remarry (line 269). Odysseus sees for himself that she is keeping to their bargain.

Despite his beggarly disguise, Odysseus, in his treatment of Irus and Eurymachus (as in his confrontation with Antinous in the previous book), shows courage and spirit. His challenge to Eurymachus (line 366ff.) that they compete in a trial of strength illustrates his indomitable and competitive character.

25 **Irus** the winged messenger of the gods is called Iris. A pun is intended in this nickname (see also line 73). His real name is Arnaeus

53 **this mischievous belly of mine** Odysseus makes much of this (compare Book 7, lines 216–17; Book 17, lines 286–9; 473–4)

85 **Echetus** a figure from folktale

125 **'You seem to be ...'** Odysseus warns Amphinomus, the most intelligent and best intentioned of the Suitors

176 **see him with a beard** crucial to the plot (see Odysseus's instructions to Penelope before he left for Troy, line 269)

221 **Look what has just happened** Penelope rebukes Telemachus: they are typically at odds with one another. Telemachus's reply shows the hastiness of Penelope's speech

277 **Such suitors bring in … expense** Penelope's soliciting of gifts appeals to Odysseus's acquisitive sense

321 **Melantho** sister of Melantheus and equally villainous

394 **he seized a stool** as Antinous had at Book 17, line 462. On this occasion, however, the taunting comes first from Eurymachus

414 **'My friends'** Amphinomus makes the peace: he is again the politic Suitor

BOOK 19   **Unrecognised, Odysseus talks to Penelope; his old nurse Eurycleia recognises him. Description of a boarhunt**

Odysseus and Telemachus remove the arms from the hall. Odysseus is insulted by Melantho again and roundly rebukes her. He talks to Penelope who tells him how she put off the Suitors with the device of the web. Odysseus tells her his Cretan tale and predicts that her husband will soon return. He is washed by Eurycleia who recognises him from the scar that he acquired in his boyhood. She is sworn to secrecy. Penelope tells the stranger of a dream which he interprets favourably. She then announces her decision to stage the contest with the bow.

> Penelope's good nature in her treatment of the stranger and her distress as she faces mounting pressures from the Suitors and from her parents to remarry are here made fully explicit. The motif of the disguise allows a full disclosure of her dilemma as she takes the stranger into her confidence. It is a test of both their characters, for Odysseus has to maintain self-control in the face of her distress.
>
> The noble **simile** in which the stranger likens Penelope's fame to that of an illustrious king (line 110ff.), whose justice is rewarded by prosperity, contrasts with Penelope's own sense of despair but raises the dignity of her character while at the same time predicting for her a just and happy outcome.
>
> After the third Cretan tale, the stranger remarks that Odysseus would have been home long ago but for his desire to travel in

pursuit of wealth: 'at accumulating wealth he is unsurpassed; in fact not a man alive can rival him' (lines 285–6). This is a frank admission of the hero's materialism from his own mouth. In his account of Odysseus's wanderings from Troy, he tactfully omits mention of Calypso.

Penelope's desire that the stranger be received with due propriety and sent upon his way with honour articulates one of the poem's principal moral values. Her comments on fame (only a good reputation can survive death; hence the impulse to excel, characteristic of the Homeric hero) are highly appropriate to her character. Her fame is praised by Odysseus here and by Agamemnon in Hades (Book 24, line 192).

Penelope's dream (line 535) is cunningly conceived by Homer. In the dream she mourns the loss of her geese, whereas for the audience it is an omen of her good fortune to come: a fine example of the **irony** that pervades the second half of the poem.

4 **we must hide ... weapon** these instructions about arms are repeated from Book 16, lines 286–94

34 **shed a beautiful light** omens and divine signs are used by Homer with increasing frequency as the climax approaches

71 **'What's got into you ...'** Odysseus rebukes Melantho: one of the great moral themes of the poem partly repeated from Book 17, lines 419–24

139 **a great web** first mentioned by Antinous at Book 2, lines 94–107

165 **an account of your family** the third Cretan tale: almost the same (in shortened form) as the fiction narrated to Eumaeus at Book 14, lines 199–359 and Antinous at Book 17, lines 415–44

173 **Crete, a rich ... land** Crete was the centre of a developed civilisation called Minoan, from the mythical king Minos, mentioned below

175 **the Achaeans ... Pelasgians** these peoples are all historical

178 **Cnossus** capital of Crete and site of famous archaeological discoveries in the late nineteenth century

187 **Malea** the most easterly promontory of the Peloponnese where Odysseus had been blown off-course in his wanderings (Book 9, line 80)

188 **Amnisus** the port of Cnossus
Eileithyie goddess of childbirth

225–35 **Noble Odysseus wore … fascinated by it** a striking picture suggesting opulence and power in marked contrast to his present condition

226 **a golden brooch** richly described and typical of the sophisticated art works represented in the Homeric poems, the most notable of which is the shield of Achilles in the *Iliad*. Note also Helen's work basket (Book 4, lines 128–32) and the doors of the palace of Alcinous (Book 7, lines 88–94). All such descriptions contribute to the impression of material beauty and splendour characteristic of the heroic age

246 **Eurybates** the description of the squire throws the beauty of Odysseus into relief

343 **having my feet washed** creature comforts are prized throughout the *Odyssey*. There is nothing Spartan (in the later sense of ascetic) about Homeric man. Here, of course, the washing advances the plot

391 **a certain scar** a celebrated episode. Odysseus later uses the scar to prove his identity to Eumaeus and Philoetius (Book 21, line 219)

409 **his name, Odysseus** *odussomai* means I hate

394 **Parnassus** a mountain above Delphi in central Greece

518 **Pandareus** a king of Crete. His daughter Aedon married Zethus king of Thebes. She had only one son Itylus. Jealous of the many children of Niobe, her sister-in-law, she planned to kill the eldest, but killed her own son by mistake. Zeus in pity changed her into a nightingale so that as such she melodiously laments the death of Itylus

524 **Am I to stay with my son** Telemachus's coming of age is the new factor pressing upon Penelope

572 **a test** the arrow is to go through twelve axes. Commentators have much debated the precise meaning of this without coming to a convincing conclusion

BOOK 20   **Prelude to the crisis with atmospheric omens. The Suitors insult Odysseus**

Odysseus witnesses the immorality of some of his maidservants as they depart to sleep with the Suitors. Odysseus is awakened by the sounds of Penelope's distress and prays for a favourable omen. Zeus thunders in a cloudless sky. Preparations begin for the festival of Apollo. Odysseus is insulted by Ctesippus who throws a cow's hoof at him. A supernatural scene at the Suitors' banquet is interpreted by

Theoclymenus to be prophetic of their doom. They carry on feasting obliviously.

At their last supper, the Suitors are seen in a most unfavourable light. Their inappropriate laughter and mockery underscore their insolence.

61 **O for an arrow** Penelope prays to Artemis for a quick release from her suffering

66 **daughters of Pandareus** apparently punished for their father's sin of stealing an artefact made by Hephaestus from the temple of Zeus in Crete

146 **Eurycleia issued her orders** she is in charge of the other female servants. Like Eumaeus she is of noble birth

185 **Philoetius** he is to help in the final encounter. In this book the effect of Odysseus's absence upon his servants is felt

210 **Cephallenian country** a neighbouring island, or possibly a general name for the surrounding area (see Book 24, lines 355; 378)

242 **a bird … on their left** a sinister omen

244 **Amphinomus** the most intelligent of the Suitors

276 **on this holy day** it is appropriate that the archery contest should take place on a day sacred to the archer god Apollo

299–300 **he laid … at him** this is the third such incident (compare Book 17, lines 462 and Book 18, line 394). This time the action is entirely unprovoked

310 **my childhood … a thing of the past** again a matter for emphasis

351 **What horror is this** Theoclymenus's vision: compare the light in the hall at Book 19, lines 33–40. But this is the only prophetic vision in the Homeric poems

BOOK 21 **Penelope brings the great bow. Odysseus reveals himself to Eumaeus. The archery contest**

Penelope descends to a storeroom to find the bow, and promises to marry the man who can string it and successfully shoot an arrow through a row of twelve axes. The axes are set up. One of the Suitors tries and fails. Odysseus reveals himself to Eumaeus and to Philoetius a loyal herdsman. When Eurymachus fails to string the bow, Antinous suggests that they postpone the contest until the following day. Odysseus asks if he can try his hand. Eumaeus brings him the bow which he successfully strings, and then shoots an arrow through the twelve axes. Telemachus arms himself and stands by his father.

The history of the bow given to him by Iphitus links Odysseus to Heracles, the greatest of all heroes, famous for his labours here mentioned. But there is a contrast, for Heracles in killing his guest violated the sacred norms of heroic society. Odysseus is a hero who upholds these norms. The contrast serves to stress the civilised nature of Odysseus as he is about to embark upon his just, if bloody, revenge.

The disquieting imagery continues when Antinous, angry that the stranger has asked for the bow, compares him to the drunken Centaur Eurytion whose unrestrained brutality provoked an equally brutal response. The warning against immoderate behaviour (line 293) is **ironic** coming from the lips of Antinous, and mention of the story is a dark foreshadowing of what is to come.

The strategic and physical preparations of Odysseus and Telemachus are detailed, well thought out and carefully executed.

6 **with her strong hand** Penelope's hand is described in the Homeric formula as *pacheie*, thick or sturdy, an **epithet** which has been thought to be inappropriate for a woman of grace and beauty

14 **Iphitus** another tale involving piracy and homicide
Eurytus a famous bowman, reputedly the teacher of Heracles

207 **'Well, here I am!'** Odysseus reveals himself to Philoetius and Eumaeus, having once again tested them just at the opportune time

295 **Eurytion the famous Centaur** the Centaurs were human to the waist and horse below it. The drunk Eurytion tried to carry off the bride at the marriage of Pirithous and Hippodamia, thus starting the battle of the Lapiths and the Centaurs

350 **So go to your quarters** Telemachus dismisses Penelope for the third time (see also Book 1, lines 346–61 and Book 17, lines 44–56). This is the strongest of his assertions at the climactic moment

391 **a ship's hawser of reeds** *biblos*, from the Egyptian papyrus from which books were later made

BOOK **22**   **The slaying of the Suitors. Penelope is told what has happened**

Odysseus kills Antinous and reveals himself to the Suitors. Eurymachus offers to make amends and begs for mercy; Odysseus kills him. Amphinomus falls to the spear of Telemachus. Father and son set about the rest of the Suitors. Through Melanthius the Suitors acquire some arms and put up some resistance. All but Phemius and Medon are killed. Eurycleia is sent for. The twelve erring maidservants are ordered to clear up the hall and then they are hanged. Melanthius is killed and mutilated. The hall is purified. Eurycleia is sent to tell Penelope of these events.

Eurymachus's speech contains a frank admission of guilt and what seems like a reasonable offer of compensation. Previously he has proved himself a smooth talker on the surface while harbouring dark motives (he continued to plot the murder of Telemachus while he reassured Penelope of his safety). The same speech in the mouth of Amphinomus, the best of the Suitors, might have made its unmerciful rejection by Odysseus seem brutal.

The presence of Athene in the guise of Mentor alongside the avengers serves to validate their cause which throughout has been accompanied by divine approval shown through omens as when Zeus thunders in a cloudless sky (Book 20, line 103) and again when Odysseus succeeds in stringing the bow (Book 21, line 413). However she does not give him a decisive victory but 'continued to put the strength and courage of both Odysseus and his noble son to the test' (line 237) so that the free will of the protagonists seems not to be compromised. They have to earn divine support.

The battle is complicated when the Suitors manage to gain access to arms. This has the effect of casting Odysseus and his friends in a more heroic light; they do not simply slaughter unarmed men.

The brutal mutilation of Melanthius (line 474) and hanging of the maidservants (line 465) are doubtless conceived on the principle that the most ignoble crime deserves the most ignoble punishment. There is **poetic justice** in the fate of Ctesippus (line 285) who had thrown a cow's hoof at Odysseus (see Book 20, line 229) and is killed by the cowman. Odysseus's speech to Medon (line 374) puts him in the role of just avenger.

It is perhaps because the Suitors' ignoble conduct renders their death a just punishment that Odysseus rebukes Eurycleia for her cry of exultation (line 411). In the *Iliad* heroes are allowed to exult over the death of an equal.

45 **Eurymachus ... tongue** the Suitors' guilt is never at issue in the poem

57 **twenty oxen** a large sum, which Laertes had paid for Eurycleia (Book 1, line 431)

205 **Athene, assuming Mentor's voice ...** Odysseus had entrusted his house to his friend Mentor on his departure (see Book 2, lines 224–8). He rebukes the people of Ithaca in the assembly for not opposing the Suitors. Athene takes his form again at the end of the poem (Book 24, line 502)

297 **her deadly aegis** probably a heavy shield with a hundred gold tassels, the means of creating panic among mortals

330 **Phemius** the priest's plea for mercy goes unheeded, but Odysseus spares the bard who promises to lay his art at his master's disposal

361 **Medon** he is lucky to escape because, although he tells Penelope of the plot against Telemachus, he also joined in the revelry (see Book 16, line 412 and Book 17, lines 172–3)

481 **sulphur** a **symbolic** as well as physical cleansing

BOOK 23   **Penelope recognises Odysseus, but tests him before sleeping with him**

Eurycleia tells Penelope what has happened. Penelope expresses disbelief, which is not dispelled when she confronts Odysseus. He is patient with her and makes plans to avoid news of the killing from reaching the outside world. After testing her husband, Penelope becomes convinced of the truth. Odysseus tells her of his wanderings, after which they spend the night together. Next morning he prepares to set off to his father's farm.

The reunion of husband and wife represents the emotional climax of the poem and the fulfilment of the 'long hope' (line 54) with which it started. Penelope's caution (foreshadowed by a similar caution in the reaction of Eumaeus) is strongly criticised by

BOOK 23 continued

Telemachus who accuses her of having a heart harder than stone (line 103). Odysseus, however, shows patience. The temper and experience of father and son are contrasted in this scene. The **ironic** misinterpretation on the part of passers-by to the sound of the music and dancing (line 149) increases sympathy for Penelope and perhaps signals Telemachus's hastiness in jumping to the wrong conclusion.

When they are alone Odysseus expresses amazement at her aloofness, which prompts her to express her amazement. Both husband and wife address each other with the same word *daemonie* which is sometimes glossed as 'strange being'. The momentary stand-off between them after a nineteen-year absence carries great psychological conviction. In her test of the bed (line 178), Penelope shows an intelligence to match that of her husband. She is the only mortal to get the better of him and to provoke him to an unconsidered outburst. Her desire for absolute certainty complements the need of Odysseus to see for himself how things are. (See Extended Commentaries, Text 3 for discussion of lines 153–208.)

Their mutual relief when they tearfully embrace is marked by a most apt **simile** (line 232), figuring the safe landing of survivors from a shipwreck. Penelope no less than Odysseus has been through seas of adversity. When she compares her position to that of Helen, she crystallises for the audience the prudence of her character and conduct by the comparison (lines 218–24).

The reunion takes place as plans are made to deal with the aftermath of the Suitor-slaying and the restoration of order in Ithaca. The wider issues of the plot are not lost sight of.

118 **When a man kills someone** the Aetolian stranger (Book 14, line 380) and Theoclymenus (Book 15, line 224) have fled their country after a homicide. Compare also the fictitious Cretan tale at Book 13, line 259. Retribution for a homicide is a matter for the kinsmen of the slain; there is no external authority. It is characteristic of Odysseus to weigh consequences

156 **Athene enhances his comeliness** repeated from Book 6, lines 230–5

228 **Actoris** not mentioned elsewhere

246 **Lampus and Phaethon** both names suggest shining light. The Dawn is drawn across the sky in a horse-drawn chariot

267 **wander on from city to city** Odysseus's final journey made partly to appease the wrath of Poseidon

310 **He began with his victory** Odysseus tells of his wanderings: a summary of his story in chronological sequence

357 **I shall repair the greater part** by plundering, evidently the customary practice in Homeric society

BOOK 24   **The Suitors' souls are guided to Hades. Odysseus is reunited with his father. They are attacked. Athene intervenes and peace is made**

Hermes escorts the Suitors' souls to Hades. The spirit of Agamemnon is surprised to see such a number and asks Amphimedon to give an account of their death. On hearing his story, Agamemnon praises Odysseus's action and extols Penelope's virtue. Odysseus visits Laertes to whom he tells a false story before finally revealing his identity to their mutual rejoicing. The Ithacans in council, after hearing of the Suitors' deaths, decide to do battle with Odysseus. Laertes, Odysseus and Telemachus begin the fight which is stopped by Athene, who commands the peace.

Penelope previously compared herself to Helen whose incautious behaviour led to countless miseries; here the climax of the interlude in Hades is Agamemnon's praise of her faithfulness and loyalty, in contrast to the treachery of his own wife Clytemnestra (line 193ff.). His prophecy that the fame of her virtue will never perish has become true. Penelope is for ever the archetype of the long-suffering faithful wife.

The reunion between Odysseus and Laertes, a figure of suffering whenever he appears in the poem, forms a **coda** to the emotional climax of the previous book and is the last of the many recognition scenes in the poem. His delight at the prospect of his son and grandson competing in valour (lines 514–15) and his active part in the campaign against the Suitors' relatives reasserts the family's control before Zeus finally concludes the peace.

1 **Cyllenian** Hermes was born on Mount Cyllene in Arcadia

2 **the ... golden wand** compare Book 5, lines 47–8. In later literature he is called *psychopompos*, the escort of souls (from *pompe* procession and *psyche* spirit or soul)

11 **the White Rock** this has occasioned much inconclusive debate; it is not referred to in other descriptions of the approach to Hades

12 **the Gates of the Sun** in the extreme west where the sun sets

15, 20 **Achilles ... Agamemnon** they are reconciled here. In the *Iliad* they are at odds

47 **Your mother** the sea-goddess Thetis

82 **Hellespont** the narrow strait between the Trojan plain and the Thracian Chersonese, now dividing Europe from Asia

87 **games in honour of their dead king** there are also funeral games for Patroclus in *Iliad* Book 23

120 **account of our tragic end** Amphimedon tells of the Suitor-slaying: he believes that Odysseus instigated the contest with the bow

129 **a great web** this is the third account. Antinous complains about Penelope's conduct in the Ithacan assembly (Book 2, lines 94–107) and Penelope tells the stranger (Book 19, lines 137–56)

378 **King of the Cephallenians** this implies all the subjects ruled by Odysseus in Ithaca and elsewhere on neighbouring islands and the mainland

377 **Nerikos** in Leucas

421 **Eupeithes** the name means plausible

482–6 **but I will tell ... prevail** Zeus calls for a happy ending: for friendship, wealth and peace

PART THREE

CRITICAL APPROACHES

The commentaries following the book by book summaries have pointed to many features of Homer's art in the management of the plot, the presentation of character, the handling of theme and the use of language. What follows here seeks to give an overall view.

PLOT

THE WELL-MADE PLOT; BEGINNING *IN MEDIAS RES*; UNITY OF ACTION

Homer tells us much of the story of Odysseus and perpetuates his fame as a traveller and wanderer, but his great skill is revealed in the most obvious feature of the structure, in his beginning *in medias res* (in the middle of things), deliberately departing from the natural chronological order of events. When he gives an account of himself to Penelope, Odysseus, in his summary of what has happened to him in the nine years since the fall of Troy, begins with his victory over the Cicones (narrated to the Phaeacians in Book 10). But Homer begins near the end of things. The main action comprising the homecoming and re-establishment of Odysseus in Ithaca takes place in a concentrated period of time amounting to little more than forty days in Odysseus's life. Hermes is despatched to free Odysseus; he makes a twenty-day journey to Scherie where he is entertained by the Phaeacians for three days and escorted back overnight to Ithaca, his journey's end coming halfway through the poem (Book 13, line 113). The rest of his nine years away from home after the fall of Troy is accounted for in a retrospective narrative that is well connected but rigorously subordinated to the main action. This artificial order enables Homer to achieve maximum concentration and **unity of action**.

Having chosen to begin at the end of Odysseus's long journey, Homer concentrates upon one single emotion, upon nostalgia in its literal meaning, upon the desire of Odysseus and of his loyal household for the hero's homecoming; for the nostalgia of Odysseus has its counterpart in the 'wish you cherished so long' of his family (Book 23, line 54) that Odysseus will one day return.

In the opening books Homer lays the groundwork for the development of his plot by introducing the characters who are the leading figures of the main action in such a way as to show how their fate and well being are entirely dependent upon Odysseus's return. Although the hero is not present in the opening, there is a great expectation of him; he is constantly in view and in the fraught situation in Ithaca we see how all depends upon his absence and upon the uncertainty surrounding his return. The sufferings of his family and household are a counterpart of the sufferings of Odysseus himself; in fact the sufferings of family and hero are two facets of a single set of circumstances united in a simple chain of cause and effect. Such is the simple unity underlying the action at the beginning of the poem.

D IVERSITY WITHIN UNITY; USE OF SETTING

Yet Homer complicates and diversifies his plot by starting with Telemachus's self-assertion and journey. He has, as it were, a double string to his bow. The self-assertion and journey are too much a part of the main design and too well integrated into the main action to constitute what could accurately be called a sub-plot. Homer's art achieves a more subtle unity. There is something very artful, too, in beginning a poem about a homecoming with a journey outwards away from home. To use a musical **metaphor**, this is a contrapuntal move. In counterpoint, which is more artful and surprising than simple melody, two tunes are combined so that they can be played together as a single theme. In interweaving the double strands of his plot Homer achieves a comparable effect.

Though it has unity of action and concentration of time the poem has diversity not unity of place. This diversity (Ithaca, Pylos, Sparta, Ogygia, Scherie and back to Ithaca) is artfully handled. The ordered worlds of Pylos and Sparta provide a real contrast to the disorderly state of Ithaca, while the land of the Phaeacians is an ideal setting for the retrospective recital of Odysseus's fabulous adventures.

Having decided to make such extensive use of old folktales (Homer could have made Odysseus's wanderings as realistic as the Cretan tales in the second half of the poem) and to isolate them in a retrospective narrative, Homer could have made Eumaeus, Telemachus or Penelope the audience for such an entertainment. Instead, he chose to have Odysseus give the recital in a world that is not unconnected with the fabulous world of the folktales. Scherie is, in fact, Odysseus's last port of call in the world of romance before he returns to the down-to-earth realities of Ithaca. There are folk motifs incorporated into the Ithacan narratives, such as the web made by Penelope and even the device of the great bow itself, but the first of these is already in the past by the time of the present action, and the second is narrated with all possible realism. The tales involving the Lotus-eaters, the Cyclops, Circe, the Sirens, and Scylla and Charybdis have more magic, mystery and romance than would have been compatible with the realistic present action in Ithaca. At the same time Scherie is nearer in a figurative as well as a literal sense to Ithaca than any other place visited by Odysseus in his wanderings. It is a fully human world in which the ideals of Greek culture are celebrated. It therefore functions as a bridge between the two orders of reality.

THE USE OF DISGUISE

Homer's narrative art is manifest in the skill with which he uses Odysseus's disguise, both as a realistic device in a credible plot and as a means of sustaining maximum human interest in his story through **ironic** effect. Odysseus reveals himself only when absolutely necessary and only to those who are to help him in the Suitor-slaying. This is the plan and it is jeopardised only when the old nurse Eurycleia almost gives the game away by telling Penelope. The disguise is the means by which Odysseus tests loyalties and finds out for himself at first hand what is actually happening in Ithaca. Hence the disguise acts as a moral test. Not only do characters prove loyal and steadfast to Odysseus but in their compassionate treatment of the apparently destitute stranger Eumaeus, Telemachus and Penelope (unlike the Suitors) prove themselves loyal to the highest moral standards of Homeric civilisation, so that the disguise comes to be the means through which the underlying morality of the poem is most effectively revealed. The disguise can therefore be said to fulfil three functions simultaneously. The first is strategic in the plot to kill the Suitors, the second is psychological in the reaction of the characters in the recognition scenes, and the third is moral in the definition and test of character and behaviour.

But there are two further artistic functions fulfilled by the disguise. Homer makes the disguised Odysseus experience at first hand the sufferings endured by his household and the iniquities perpetrated by the Suitors. Our sympathies are firmly enlisted on the side of the hero and against the Suitors with every insult and injury he suffers, so that in the Suitors' richly deserved punishment the interests of poetic justice are firmly upheld. Homer's second strategy is to enrich his plot with as many recognition scenes as possible. The first occurs when Odysseus recognises Ithaca and then the goddess in disguise (Book 13). Then comes the recognition of father and son (Book 16), followed by recognition of master and faithful dog (Book 17), master and old nurse (Book 19), master and faithful retainer (Book 22), the climactic recognition of husband and wife (Book 23), and finally the recognition of son and father (Book 24). We can see that it might well be expedient for Odysseus to keep Penelope in the dark, but of course Homer wants the great recognition scene between husband and wife to be delayed to a point at which it has maximum effect. All these recognition scenes are full of **pathos** and psychological interest. The three most poignant naturally involve Odysseus in his closest relations. Through them Homer celebrates the most basic natural bonds of human life between parent and child and, above all, between husband and wife.

THE DIVINE MACHINERY

Homer's manipulation of his **divine machinery** serves to clarify the main outline of the plot so that the audience is free to concentrate not so much upon what will happen next but upon how it will happen. As to what will happen, the ultimate issue is never in doubt. Athene in the disguise of Mentor predicts the Suitors' doom at the end of Book 2. The audience is told the story; the surprise and suspense are related not to the ultimate outcome but to the manner in which it is brought about. Through the utterances and interventions of the gods the audience sees the human action from an Olympian point of view.

A council of the gods is a convenient way of setting the poem in motion. Athene rebukes Zeus for hostility to Odysseus. Zeus protests in reply that it is Poseidon who hates Odysseus because he had blinded his son Polyphemus the Cyclops. As Zeus expresses no objection to Odysseus's homecoming, Athene proposes to send Hermes to Ogygia to free him and to send Telemachus to Sparta and Pylos to look for Odysseus, an enterprise that will redound to his credit. In the council of the gods in Book 5 Zeus despatches Hermes to Ogygia, telling the exact course of his twenty-day journey to Scherie and the circumstances of his return in a brief summary of the action from Books 5 to 13. In Book 13 Athene arranges the disguise of Odysseus and helps plan the Suitors' destruction in which she promises to take part. In the fight she appears with her aegis. In the final lines of the poem, Zeus and Athene, like the *deus ex machina* in Greek tragedy, solve the problem of continuing resistance to Odysseus by intervening to prevent further bloodshed.

In every human action the gods are involved. Athene guards and guides Telemachus. She sends a phantom sister to comfort Penelope. She puts the idea for the expedition to wash clothes in Nausicaa's head and enshrouds Odysseus in mist as he makes his way to the palace. In all this we may regard the goddess herself as cause and instigator, with her own reasons for promoting the action. These reasons can be part of the overall chain of cause and effect. Or, since she is the goddess of wisdom and associated with the mind, we may feel that, when she puts ideas into characters' heads, this is Homer's way of arranging for them to make decisions. The divine presence magnifies the protagonists, but it also identifies the gods with Odysseus's cause, as do the various divine signs apparent in the poem. In the first Ithacan council, Zeus sends an omen, which the soothsayer interprets as spelling doom to the Suitors. Through the soothsayer's prophecy Homer gives a brief summary of the whole of his plot. Just before the final reckoning, Odysseus prays to Zeus to send a sign if it is true that he has been guided on his homeward journey by the gods. Zeus obligingly thunders in a cloudless sky. This follows Penelope's account of the dream in which an eagle destroys a flock of geese, which has clear reference to Odysseus's forthcoming destruction of the Suitors. Penelope mistrusts the dream but the audience know better. Divine interventions and signs interact with prophecies and dreams; they help to give shape to the narrative and to propel it forward, to heighten tension, and to suggest an underlying fate, unseen but inevitable, gradually being brought to fruition in the outcome of the action.

CHARACTER

The purely functional character is exemplified in the person of Mentor who has given his name to what he represents in the *Odyssey*: an experienced guardian or guide. All the characters have a clear function in relation to the main action. Odysseus is the just and responsible king who is to restore order to Ithaca on his return. Around him we can see the dutiful son, the loyal wife, the faithful retainer and the good old nurse, and in opposition to him the wicked Suitors. But the *Odyssey* would have been a very flat tale if this were all. Homer has given the world a gallery of fully rounded characters who have an imaginative appeal that transcends the poem in which they occur. This is particularly true of Odysseus himself, who has exerted a fascination on subsequent readers comparable to that of Shakespeare's Hamlet. To a large extent this is a consequence of his dramatic presentation; characters are established not by authorial pronouncement but by their own words and deeds.

THE SUITORS

The Suitors, like Odysseus's companions, are constantly referred to *en masse*. As Odysseus's companions take no part in the main action Homer does not concern himself with their characterisation. But in the case of the Suitors he has carefully distinguished three quite different forms of iniquity.

Antinous their leader, whose very name suggests one who is antagonistic (compared with *Alcinous's* name which suggests strength of mind), is straightforwardly a nasty piece of work. All his speeches are direct, insulting and without disguise. As leader of the gang he initiates the plot against Telemachus in the beginning and renews it later when it has misfired. He angrily insults the disguised Odysseus and refuses to give him food when he begs for it, throwing a footstool at him instead. For this gross breach of the sacred Greek custom of hospitality he is rebuked even by his fellow Suitors. Through him Homer represents the Suitors' behaviour in its ugliest aspect. All his speeches and actions point to this end.

Eurymachus seems altogether a more genial fellow. In contrast to Antinous's anger and emotion, he makes a soothing speech to Telemachus at the opening, assuring him of their good intentions (Book 1, lines 400–11). In the council, though he is stern with the soothsayer, he nevertheless does not blame Penelope at length as Antinous does, but puts more emphasis upon the apparently reasonable solution that Telemachus should send Penelope back to her father's house (Book 2, lines 194–207). Homer in the beginning does not implicate him directly by name in the plot against Telemachus. Later we hear that he is the favoured choice of Penelope's father and brothers (Book 15, line 17). Telemachus even advises Theoclymenus to go to Eurymachus's house where he can expect to meet a more orderly reception than in his own home (Book 15, line 518). When Penelope rebukes the Suitors for plotting against her son, it is Eurymachus who makes a soothing speech assuring her of his protection for her son whom he regards as the dearest of men. He speaks to encourage her (and to gain her good opinion) while 'death for Telemachus was in his heart' (Book 16, line 448). Later he flatters Penelope, praising her beauty when she appears before the Suitors to elicit gifts from them (Book 18, lines 245–9). While Antinous exhibited simple anger at the beggar, Eurymachus at first makes jokes about his baldness and ugliness to ridicule him and is only driven to anger and the use of a footstool when Odysseus has provoked him in return. When Odysseus finally reveals himself, Eurymachus admits the Suitors' iniquities and tries to shift all the blame on to Antinous. All in all, he is a more subtle character than Antinous, with a more attractive exterior masking hidden cunning. His iniquity is more hypocritical and disguised.

Amphinomus, Penelope's favourite among the Suitors, who still has some inherent goodness (Book 16, lines 397–8), recognises the iniquity of the plot against Telemachus when it has miscarried and diverts the Suitors' thoughts away from further action (Book 16, lines 400–5). He greets the beggar at the feast and wishes him good fortune. When the disguised Odysseus issues his warning, he is heavy at heart and filled with foreboding (Book 18, lines 153–5). His guilt, in contrast to the insensitivity of Antinous or the hypocrisy of Eurymachus, is strongly felt in this scene. After Eurymachus has been provoked to throw a stool at Odysseus, Amphinomus urges reverence towards Telemachus's guest and makes the peace (Book 18, lines 412–21). Nevertheless, it is his doom, pronounced by Athene (Book 18, lines 155–6), to die alongside the rest. Homer leaves us to draw our own conclusions.

The character of Antinous is constant throughout the action, that of Eurymachus is gradually revealed by the action, and that of Amphinomus is introduced at a moment in the action when the issue of guilt comes to the fore. These three characters are clearly differentiated in a realistic way that is quite consistent in each individual case. Their reactions and behaviour together are varied and make up an interesting pattern of diversity credible within the group. This is a source of great human interest in the plot; the Suitors are not mere ciphers.

Furthermore, however simple the broad moral outline of the poem may be, the Suitors are allowed a point of view. In the initial speech to the assembly in which Antinous puts all the blame on Penelope for promising one thing and performing another, there is some justice. The whole situation has the complexity of real life, particularly when, as a result of the point of departure *in medias res*, there is some difficulty in unravelling the threads of the knotty problem that Homer has presented us with at the beginning of the poem.

Nor is all the Suitors' behaviour equally outrageous. There is displeasure at Antinous's refusal to give alms, for example, and another of the Suitors called Agelaus makes a conciliatory speech full of good sense after Telemachus has complained of their treatment of the beggar (Book 20, lines 322–37). That Homer's villains should be susceptible to better feelings and right behaviour is a further example of his skill as a storyteller, since their better moments serve only to emphasise the violation of Greek manners represented by their general behaviour. Despite Agelaus's speech, the description of their last supper concludes with laughter and raillery at the beggar's expense.

TELEMACHUS

In the case of Telemachus the initial course of the action is grounded in his self-assertion now that he has come of age. The self-assertion is what finally causes Penelope to initiate the contest with the bow. Odysseus had told her to leave his house and marry again (if he had not returned) when their son had grown a beard on his chin (Book 18, lines 269–70). It is not the physical fact of his coming of age that moves Penelope, but the proof that he is now becoming a power in his own right. At the beginning of the poem, when she complains about Phemius's song, Telemachus orders her to go to her chamber, whereupon she shows great surprise (Book 1, lines 345–61). The motif is repeated later when he tells his mother that he will give the bow to whom he wishes, and bids her retire (Book 21, lines 344–55). The Suitors are similarly surprised by his speeches in the assembly which he has called, by his ability to bring off the proposed journey, and by his sternness towards them when he has returned to the palace. At the opening of the poem, Athene, in disguise, admonishes Telemachus that few sons are worthy of their fathers; Orestes is held up as an example of a son who well served the interests of his father (Book 1, lines 296–302; Book 2, lines 276–8). In the course of the poem Telemachus is to prove himself worthy. He passes the various tests that are laid for him, and, in the second half of the poem, shows the self-control that he had not quite managed earlier when he burst into tears in the assembly. He almost strings the bow, proves himself adept in the final encounter, and Laertes rejoices to see his son and grandson vying with each other in valour (Book 24, lines 513–15).

ODYSSEUS

It is on the character of Odysseus that the action principally turns. The essence of his characterisation in Homer is simple and clear, and is indicated in the various **epithets** given to him. In the opening line of the poem he is said to be *polytropos*, variously translated as the man of many ways, many turns or many parts. He is also *polymetis* and *polymechanos*, the man of much contrivance and many devices, and of course *polytlas*, much suffering and enduring. All four epithets are united by the prefix *poly*, representing him as the man of great experience who has seen cities and known the minds of men. His knowledge of the world based on experience is matched by his experience of the world – he has done, achieved and suffered many things – from which he has learned.

Homer's polytropic hero and his polytropic plot reflect each other perfectly. Odysseus's character unfolds naturally with the action. His absence at the start creates a great expectation of him which is fuelled by the reminiscences of Nestor, Helen and Menelaus. In the plot these reminiscences also serve as anticipations. For Nestor, recalling the heroic enterprise of the campaign now long since past, Odysseus was the master strategist (Book 3, line 120). Nestor the sage old counsellor found in Odysseus a kindred spirit, sharing his political sense. They never spoke at variance in the Achaeans' assembly. Menelaus, a man of action himself, recalls the man of action who did more on behalf of the Greek cause at Troy than anyone else (Book 4, lines 106–7). Helen, herself a subtle figure, tells the story of the clever ruse through which Odysseus entered Troy disguised as a beggar, on a mission of intelligence (Book 3, lines 240–56). Menelaus then tells of Odysseus's behaviour inside the Wooden Horse when he had the presence of mind to keep the Greeks from revealing themselves. He also comments on Odysseus's physical prowess in wrestling. These anticipations all help to raise a vivid idea of the polytropic hero in the audience's imagination.

On Calypso's isle Odysseus first enters the poem as the long-suffering hero, alone and tearful. When Calypso tells him she will help him to leave, he mistrusts her, requiring a solemn oath that she is not plotting his ruin. The nymph is amused at the suspicious nature of Odysseus's crafty mind. In making the raft he shows himself to be practical, resourceful and a good craftsman. In the storm we see the heroic spirit of Odysseus recoiling from the horror of a death at sea, wishing instead that like Achilles he could have died on the plains of Troy, a death that would have spread his fame abroad. In the sea Homer shows him to be constantly using his wits to extricate himself from trouble. Once on land he collects himself and in his interview with Nausicaa shows a tact and delicacy of feeling that puts him in an altogether new light. His concern for her reputation is sensitive and civilised. At the palace his tact in dealing with the Phaeacians is politic but also decent in itself. When provoked he proves his physical excellence in the games. Declaring his identity at the opening of his retrospective narrative he announces that he is known among men for all manner of stratagems: his fame reaches the heavens (Book 9, line 19). The word always associated with him and which he uses here is *dolos*: wiles, craft, stratagem, cunning. The account of his adventures reveals him to be the wily Greek who has been tested in a wide variety of experiences. When he has landed in 'Ithaca, he craftily invents his first Cretan tale to conceal his identity from the young shepherd who is Athene in disguise. When the goddess reveals herself, she is amused at his cunning and inventiveness and his delight in lying tales. He does not immediately trust her, suspecting that she is beguiling him. Athene finds this very much in character, a character to which she is akin herself. She call him *epetes*, *agkinoos* and *echephron* (Book 13, line 332). These words all refer to qualities of mind. The first seems related to *epos* (word) and is variously translated as soft or fluent of speech or civilised; Odysseus certainly has a way with words. The second is intelligent or of quick understanding; he is always quick to sum up a situation and to grasp an opportunity. The third is having understanding, self-possession, control, prudence; he generally shows great presence of mind. It is striking that this characterisation comes after these qualities have been fully demonstrated in the action and that it is put into the mouth of another character rather than delivered through direct authorial comment. These are the qualities of mind and character by virtue of which Odysseus has succeeded so far and they will be necessary if he is to succeed in repossessing his own house.

The rest of the plot is a test and display of these aspects of the hero's character. It shows his supreme *dolos*. His inventiveness is apparent in his devising credible tales which are always well adapted to the speaker and his audience. His quickness of mind is apparent throughout as he takes advantage of every opportunity, particularly in the way he encourages Penelope to arrange for the contest with the bow. As a strategist he is cautious, testing character and planning in advance, as when he removes the armour from the hall. His self-control is evident in the way in which he sustains his disguise without giving himself away before he judges it to be expeditious either to those loyal to him or to his enemies. All of this requires that he be a consummate actor, confident in his role and adequate to meet all aspects of the situation confronting him – the true polytropic hero.

That Odysseus emerges as all-round and three-dimensional is a consequence of the way in which he is presented in Homer. It is not only that we see him in the many different roles that a man may be called upon to play – father, husband, son, master, lover, comrade-in-arms, politician, avenger, the list is a long one – but we also see him from many different points of view. Each point of view has ground for support in the action itself. His mother Anticleia, for example, singles out his gentleness, and this aspect of his character (which does not exclude its opposite, for Odysseus can be stern and fierce) is evident in his dealings with Nausicaa and in the sensitivity shown to Penelope in the latter part of the poem. Homer even allows a critical view. To Eurylochus, Odysseus's adventures with the Cyclops and Circe illustrate his reckless disregard for the safety of his companions (Book 10, lines 431–7). Different aspects of his character, overlapping and shading into one another but with a distinctly individual point of view, are given in the varied testimonies of Nestor, Helen, Menelaus, Anticleia, Athene, Penelope, Eumaeus, Eurycleia and Laertes. At the same time these testimonies tell something of the character of those who give them, so that they are only partial accounts, aspects and facets of the man as he appears to those who know him. As a result of this dramatic representation, the portrayal of Odysseus is multi-faceted and true to life. There is no one fixed stable point of view enforced by an omniscient narrator, with the exception of what is given in the **epithets** long-suffering and polytropic.

Odysseus appears to be a true-to-life character because of the perspective adopted upon his life in the form of the poem itself. This perspective is the larger aspect of points of view discussed above. Homer concentrates upon about forty days in his life. Of his future we hear a brief prophecy from Teiresias, and his past – going back as far as his early youth – is contained in the reminiscences of Eurycleia and Laertes. The *Odyssey* has the breadth of a great chronicle but with none of its limitations and restrictions. We are allowed a telescopic view but from a fixed point of time. The *Odyssey* gives a representation of a vivid extended present, highlights of the past and a brief intimation of the future. This in itself is a satisfying and credible form in which to present the imitation of life, since it is universal. This is how we all experience time in which it seems that we are always *in medias res* or near the end of things. The *Odyssey* does not purport to tell us the whole truth about Odysseus, but to present the significant truth of forty days of his experience. In spite of that we do have a broad and telescopic view of his character over a greater period of time. Homer has concentration and breadth in ideal proportions. In his modern novel *Ulysses*, James Joyce deals with eighteen hours in the life of a contemporary man. Such intense concentration puts that life under a microscope in such a way that we lose a sense of overall form and coherence because of the perspective adopted. This perspective may be equally or more true to life. The simple point of contrast here is that Homer's perspective allows us to grasp the character and experience of Odysseus in some depth without losing coherence in detail. Homer presents life and character not in all its bewildering complexity but in a form in which we can see meaning and pattern.

PENELOPE

Penelope's character is celebrated throughout the *Odyssey*. Her faithfulness and steadfastness are contrasted with Clytemnestra's disloyalty which proved to be Agamemnon's undoing. In Hades Agamemnon's spirit, after recounting his wife's iniquity, tells Odysseus that there is no danger of his suffering a similar fate, as Penelope is too intelligent and understanding (Book 11, lines 444–6). In the final book, Agamemnon's spirit again pronounces judgement upon Penelope: 'The glory of her virtue (*arete*) will not fade with the years, but the deathless gods themselves will make a beautiful song for mortal ears in honour of the constant Penelope' (*echephron* – having understanding, prudence, self-possession: Book 24, lines 196–8). There is a fine **decorum** in this judgement. It acquires more authority from Agamemnon's lips than if it had been delivered by Odysseus or by the narrator. (Indeed the whole Agamemnon story is woven into the *Odyssey* with great skill.) Odysseus's character is subtle and not without complexity, given his role as the polytropic hero in a polytropic poem. But Penelope's virtue is pre-eminent and unequivocal. It is manifested in her constancy and suggested by the **epithet** given to her by Agamemnon and repeated throughout the poem. Nevertheless, she is not a flat character. She is most sensitively presented; we see her suffering spirit under threat and always on the defensive. She has used her wits, and successfully outwitted the Suitors for three years with the stratagem of the web. Faced with the stranger claiming to be Odysseus, she is cautious and sceptical. Her caution has become proverbial. Telemachus thinks she is overstubborn. She turns the tables on Odysseus and tests him with a stratagem of her own devising concerning their marriage bed. When she finally yields, she apologises to Odysseus, telling him of her fear that she might be deceived by a plausible stranger. She then calls to mind the example of Helen who, though she would never have slept with her foreign love, if she could have foreseen the disastrous consequences of her action, nevertheless succumbed to a momentary infatuation (Book 23, lines 218–24). We may recall here Nestor's remark that Clytemnestra was a perfectly good woman until prevailed upon by her paramour (Book 3, lines 265–6). Penelope's scepticism and caution are aspects of her intelligence and control. Given the dilemma in which she finds herself, they are perfectly reasonable and are elements of a credible psychological unity. The prominence of her virtue in the poem is one of the reasons (another is the prominence of Arete in the Phaeacian episode) that led the English Victorian writer Samuel Butler (1835–1902) to believe that the Odyssey had been composed by a woman.

SUPPORTING ROLES

The role of *Eumaeus*, the good and faithful steward, is to afford shelter to Odysseus. He is straightforward, plain-speaking, pious and dutiful. In the humble setting of his hut, his frugal ways are contrasted with the arrogant profligacy of the Suitors in the palace. In his entertainment of the indigent stranger he exhibits good sense, tolerance, sensitivity and tact that are indicative of true nobility, something that transcends position and fortune in life (though Eumaeus is of noble origin). The good pigman is something of a moral touchstone and his role has some of the **symbolic** force of the good shepherd in the Christian story. He is, nevertheless, a fully realistic character, very much associated with his setting and with the ordinary activities of his day-to-day life.

Similarly *Eurycleia*, the old nurse, is usually busy with the activities of housekeeping. She is made to serve a very different purpose. She is a good woman but her role has little symbolic force. Homer uses her memorably in the sequence of recognition scenes where her reaction of tumultuous enthusiasm (she upsets the washtub) almost gives the game away. Her cry of triumph after the Suitor-slaying serves to make a moral point. It is not holy, says Odysseus, to exult over the deaths of the unworthy.

Laertes, a lonely and impotent figure of suffering in the absence of his son, is restored to active well being in the final moments of the poem. Before Athene commands the peace, Odysseus exhorting Telemachus to do battle with the Ithacan opposition expresses confidence that he will not shame the house of their fathers which has always been foremost in valour and strength. As one of those fathers, Laertes rejoices in the competing strength of his son and grandson. In Laertes's joy, the regeneration of the house of Odysseus is thus completed.

While characters all have their individual parts to play within the action and their own particular behavioural traits to exhibit, integration is achieved through their subtle interaction and the ways they can be said to support one another. Crucial qualities of mind and character are reduplicated through a variety of parts. Athene remarks on the close natural affinity between herself and Odysseus. Like him she is a subtle spirit who delights in dissimulation and disguise. He is her favourite because he excels in the human sphere in all the qualities of mind and character for which she is known among the gods (Book 13, lines 297–8). Odysseus is the master of wiles and trickery, but Penelope, in the stratagem of the web and in her test of Odysseus, exhibits a comparable guile and craft. Penelope's caution finds an echo in her husband's behaviour with Calypso and Athene, and as the beggar in disguise. In both cases it is an aspect of their good sense and control, as evidenced in the epithet *echephron* (prudent) given to them both. Telemachus may be inexperienced but he is no fool and frequently merits the epithet *pepnumenos* – of sound understanding. When father and son plot the destruction of the Suitors he gives good advice modifying his father's plans (Book 16, lines 309–20). He has to use his wits and show self-control in his treatment of the Suitors. In the crucial moment, it is through his firm intervention that Odysseus is finally given the bow. He is conceived very much in his father's mould, and proves adequate to his supporting role because of qualities of character that he shares with his father. That characters should reinforce each other in this way lends realism and credibility to the plot. It also results in artistic cohesion. The qualities of mind and character which are vindicated in the action and through its outcome are manifested not only in the central character but are reinforced by their pervading presence in the poem as a whole.

MAJOR THEMES

JUSTICE, ORDER & RIGHT CONDUCT

Zeus at the very beginning expresses concern that mortals blame the gods for their problems when in reality they bring them upon themselves through their own transgressions. In the narrative of the wanderings it is clear that Odysseus's companions perish through their own witlessness and folly in killing the oxen of the Sun, despite repeated warnings and their own solemn oath that they would not do so. In the larger action, the Suitors perish because of their greed and wickedness. In wasting the substance of another man's house they flagrantly breach Homeric manners. Their behaviour shows a lack of shame or restraint, all that is implied in the Homeric word *aidos*. Predicting their doom, Athene specifically says that they are witless and unjust (Book 2, line 282). With their profligacy in mind, the good Eumaeus remarks: 'the blessed gods don't like wicked acts. Justice and fair play are what they respect in men.' (Book 14, lines 83–4) Their plot to kill Telemachus goes beyond a breach of acceptable social behaviour to downright wickedness. They meet their just deserts at the hand of Odysseus whose just vengeance punishes that wickedness and in so doing sets the scene for the re-establishment of moral order in his own house. The Homeric norm represented by the stable and just households of Nestor at Pylos and Menelaus at Sparta (both Nestor and Menelaus condemn the Suitors when told about them by Telemachus), and the orderly world of the Phaeacians, can now be reasserted in Ithaca.

HOSPITALITY TO THE VISITING STRANGER

Propriety in the treatment of the visiting stranger is a persistent moral imperative and the great test of moral character in the *Odyssey*. The most conspicuous failure to honour this fundamental constituent of the civilised Homeric code occurs when the savage Cyclops eats his guests instead of feeding them. Otherwise it is universally acknowledged even when it is breached.

When Athene visits Odysseus's palace in mortal guise, Telemachus is the first to notice her and he feels shame that a stranger should wait long at the gates: 'Welcome friend!' he said. 'You can tell us what has brought you here when you have had some food.' (Book 1, lines 123–4)

Both Nestor and Menelaus welcome Telemachus unconditionally before they know his identity. The same courtesy is extended to Odysseus as a visiting stranger by the Phaeacian king and queen. Visitors are not only entertained but sent away with a parting gift. Telemachus is given a chariot and horses by Nestor for his journey to Sparta, whence he departs with a silver mixing bowl made by Hephaestus and given to him by Menelaus. Odysseus leaves Phaeacia loaded with a quantity of treasure.

Addressing the shipwrecked Odysseus on his arrival in Phaeacia, Nausicaa remarks that fortune or misfortune is determined by Zeus, before reassuring her maidservants and reminding them of their duty: 'This man is an unfortunate wanderer who has strayed here, and we must look after him, since all strangers and beggars come under the protection of Zeus' (Book 6, lines 206–8). This is a sentiment much repeated when Odysseus is in disguise as a beggar in Ithaca. Eumaeus, Telemachus and Penelope welcome the stranger unconditionally and prove their moral worth by so doing. When Odysseus begs amongst the Suitors he reminds them of this duty and he is not refused food, but he is, nevertheless, maltreated by some of their number. The strength of the imperative to extend courteous treatment even to the indigent is apparent when, even from amongst the Suitors, there is a protest when Antinous strikes the disguised Odysseus (Book 17, lines 481–7). Telemachus expresses regret that he cannot give Theoclymenus the welcome he would like, as does Penelope to the disguised stranger.

LANGUAGE & STYLE

For features of the Homeric oral style see Background, on The Language of Homer.

The *Odyssey*'s epic style (using a broad understanding of the word style) entails a number of formal features that it shares with the *Iliad*. Characters, places and things are dignified with formal **epithets**: Zeus is 'the Gatherer of the Clouds'; Athene is 'the goddess with the flashing eyes' and 'the daughter of Zeus who bears the aegis'; Hermes is 'the keen eyed Giant-slayer'; Dawn is 'rosy-fingered'; Odysseus is 'godlike', 'much suffering' and 'much contriving'; Penelope is 'fair' and 'wise'; Ithaca is 'rugged'; Pylos is the 'well-built citadel of Neleus'; ships are 'swift' and 'black'; the sea is 'wine dark'; words are 'winged'. Characters address each other with some formality in set speeches. Objects are described in terms of their history, as in the case of the bow. There are many mythological allusions and extended **similes**.

Mythological allusions relate the narrative to other famous stories, which not only diversifies but also can confirm the heroic character of the narrative. In the history of the bow, for example, there is an allusion to Heracles, a son of Zeus famous for his Twelve Labours. The bow is said to have been given to the young Odysseus by Iphitus, who subsequently met his death at the hands of Heracles. The allusion indirectly associates Odysseus with the most famous of all heroes of achievement but also suggests a contrast: 'For Heracles killed him in his own house, though he was Iphitus' host, caring no more in that cruel heart of his for the vengeful eye of the gods than for the hospitality he had given him' (Book 21, lines 26–9). Odysseus is raised in the imagination by the comparison which marks him out as a god-fearing upholder of civilised values. The effect of allusions to other characters and stories celebrated in myth is, therefore, often subtle. When Odysseus expresses his desire to attempt the stringing of the bow, Antinous angrily invokes the example of Eurytion the Centaur, whose drunken attempt to seize the bride of Pirithous started the bloody battle of the Lapiths and Centaurs, to warn off Odysseus (Book 21, lines 293–304). This **ironic** reference (since we know that Odysseus is not drunk and that a violent end is about to be visited upon the Suitors) has the effect of associating their own profligate and excessive behaviour with that of the Centaurs themselves.

Most of the similes do not feature figures or stories from myth but give little pictures of everyday life. Their intrinsic charm is often intensified by the artful way in which they are integrated into the surrounding narrative. For example, when Odysseus returns to his ship, after he has mastered Circe and freed his companions whom she had turned into pigs, his remaining companions greet him with tearful joy: 'It was like the scene at a farm when cows in a drove come home full-fed from the pastures to the yard and are welcomed by all their frisking calves, who burst out from the pens to gambol round their mothers, lowing excitedly' (Book 10, lines 410–14). Here the joyful animal simile has a particular piquancy coming after the metamorphosis of his men. Similarly there is great irony and appropriateness when Eumaeus in the presence of the disguised Odysseus greets Telemachus on his return: 'Like a fond father welcoming back his son after nine years abroad, his only son, the apple of his eye for whom he has sacrificed much, the admirable swineherd threw his arms round Telemachus the godlike youth and showered kisses on him as though he had just escaped from death' (Book 16, lines 17–21). The irony is intensified by the last clause, for the audience know, what the characters do not, that Telemachus has indeed just escaped ambush at the hands of the Suitors. The similes and their imagery have immediate point but can also carry thematic significance and reverberate against the larger narrative in which they occur.

A distinctive feature of Homer's style in the *Odyssey* as opposed to the *Iliad* is the inclusion of low or common details that have sometimes been thought to be below the dignity of an **epic** poem. The simile in which the hero on the eve of the Suitor-slaying, kept awake by his anxiety as to which plan to adopt, is likened to a black pudding being turned this way and that on the fire (Book 20, lines 25–7) is a notorious example. Odysseus has just witnessed the immorality of the Suitors making merry at his expense and retiring to sleep with his maidservants. Epic dignity is appropriate when the subject matter of the epic is dignified; 'low' vocabulary and imagery occur in low contexts and can always be defended on the grounds of internal artistic **decorum**.

Imagery in the poem is always appropriate to character, setting and theme. This may be illustrated from three differing parts of the narrative. Odysseus's encounter with Nausicaa comes after the turbulent narrative of his shipwreck. The change of mood and scene is marked by the extended description of the tranquil Olympus, the everlasting abode of the gods, to which Athene retires (Book 6, lines 41–7), followed immediately by the Dawn that awakens the young princess Nausicaa. The narrative continues with the account of the washing expedition followed by the game of ball which she plays with her maidservants. Then comes a simile which raises her in the imagination by likening her pre-eminence among the group of young girls to that of the goddess Artemis when she joyfully hunts game with her wood nymphs in attendance (Book 6, lines 102–9). Into this scene of chaste playful beauty comes the gnarled and near naked Odysseus, likened to a weather-beaten mountain lion driven by hunger to attack the cattle or sheep (Book 6, lines 130–4). The simile makes a dramatic contrast and perfectly reflects the hero's condition. Though we may be sure that he has no malign intentions towards the young girls, the simile also makes the danger of the situation from their point of view very clear without actually spelling it out, and further emphasises Nausicaa's courage in facing Odysseus. She is truly worthy of the comparison to the fearless goddess. In view of the previous imagery, Odysseus's opening words of address, likening her to the goddess Artemis, are highly appropriate and extend the impression of her beauty and purity. His comparison of her beauty to that of a young palm tree growing by the altar of Apollo at Delos, with all its sacred associations, further endows her natural beauty with a supernatural aura (Book 6, line 162ff.). The imagery relating to Nausicaa makes apparent the nature of her beauty and magnifies it through comparison to the divine.

In the account of the Suitor-slaying, the imagery, mostly drawn from the animal world, reflects and intensifies the violence and brutality of the action. The Suitors are like cattle stung by the gadfly, while those attacking them are likened to vultures swooping down on smaller birds (Book 22, lines 229–306). At the end of the slaughter, the Suitors are likened to quantities of fish cast out of meshes to lie on the sand gasping for life (Book 22, lines 384–8). Odysseus is like a lion covered with blood after feeding on a farmer's bullock (Book 22, lines 402–5). The maidservants are hanged like doves or thrushes caught in nets as they come home to roost (Book 22, lines 468–70).

Imagery surrounding Penelope is dignified and poignant. The disguised Odysseus makes a magnificent tribute to her virtue by telling her that her fame has reached heaven itself

> like that of a some illustrious king, ruling a populous and mighty country with the fear of the gods in his heart, and upholding justice. As a result of his good leadership the dark soil yields its wheat and barley, the trees are laden with ripe fruit, the sheep never fail to bear their lambs, nor the sea to provide its fish; and his people prosper under him. (Book 19, lines 109–14)

The image may be masculine, but it is one of a richly beneficent power that raises Penelope's status in the audience's imagination and indirectly provides a poignant contrast with her current state in Ithaca. After she has finally yielded to her husband, and they tearfully embrace:

It was like the moment when the blissful land is seen by struggling sailors, whose fine ship Poseidon has battered with wind and wave and smashed on the high seas. A few swim safely to the mainland out of the foaming surf, their bodies caked with brine; and blissfully they tread on solid land, saved from disaster. It was bliss like that for Penelope to see her husband once again. (Book 23, lines 233–9)

In this simile the poet honours Penelope too, for although it clearly fits the experience of her husband it is to his wife that it is primarily applied. Penelope, no less than Odysseus, has been through seas of adversity. The simile in fact embraces them both as they embrace, celebrating their mutual relief and endurance with wonderful appropriateness.

Many of the images in the poem are beautiful or vivid in themselves but it is perhaps their decorum, their appropriateness, the way in which they are artfully fitted into the surrounding narrative and re-echo its major themes that constitute their chief beauty, an artistic beauty that can embrace all the imagery even when the pictures are ugly in themselves.

PART FOUR

EXTENDED COMMENTARIES

TEXT 1   (BOOK 8, LINES 487–547)

'Demodocus, I admire you above all men. Either Zeus' Child, the Muse, or Apollo must have been your teacher. For it is remarkable how accurately you sing the tale of the Achaeans' fate and of all their achievements, sufferings and struggles. It is almost as though you had been with them yourself or heard the story from one who was. But now change your theme and sing to us of the stratagem of the Wooden Horse, which Epeius built with Athene's help, and which the good Odysseus contrived to get taken one day into the citadel of Troy as an ambush, manned by the warriors who then sacked the town. If you can tell this as it really happened I shall proclaim to the world how generously the god has endowed you with the heavenly gift of song.'

Odysseus finished speaking, and the bard, beginning with an invocation to the gods, unfolded the tale. He took it up at the point where the Argives after setting fire to their huts had embarked on their ships and were sailing away, while the renowned Odysseus and his party were already sitting in the assembly-place in Troy, concealed within the Horse, which the Trojans had themselves dragged into the citadel. There stood the Horse, with the Trojans sitting round it endlessly arguing. Three policies commended themselves. Some were for piercing the wooden frame with a pitiless bronze spear; others would have dragged it to the edge of the heights and hurled it down the rocks; others again wished to let it stand as a magnificent offering to appease the gods – and that was what happened in the end. For it was destiny that they should perish when Troy received within her walls that mighty Wooden Horse, laden with the flower of the Argive might bringing doom and slaughter to the Trojans.

He went on to sing how the Achaean warriors, leaving their hollow ambush, poured out from the Horse to ravage Troy; how they scattered through the steep streets of the city leaving ruin in their wake; and how Odysseus, looking like Ares himself, went straight to Deiphobus' house with the gallant Menelaus. And there, sang the bard, he engaged in the most terrible of all his fights, which in the end he won with the help of the indomitable Athene.

While the famous minstrel was singing, Odysseus' heart was melting with grief and his cheeks were wet with the tears that ran down from his eyes. He wept as a woman weeps when she throws her arms round the body of her beloved husband, fallen in battle in the defence of his city and his comrades, fighting to save his city and his children from the evil day. She has found him gasping in the throes of death; she clings to him wailing and lamenting. But the enemy come up and beat her back and shoulders with spears, as they lead her off into slavery and a life of miserable toil, with her cheeks wasted by her pitiful grief. Equally pitiful were the tears that now welled up in Odysseus' eyes, and though he succeeded in hiding them from everyone else, Alcinous could not help observing his condition; he was sitting next to him and heard his heavy groans.

Having arrived at the palace of the Phaeacians, Odysseus is entertained by them and competes in their games. In the course of the entertainment, Demodocus, whose name means 'honoured of the people' sings first of the quarrel of Odysseus and Achilles and then of the loves of Ares and Aphrodite. After an evening banquet, Odysseus now makes his request. His expression of admiration for the bard is repeated when he begins his own tale of his wanderings (Book 9, line 7). This admiration may be regarded as reflecting Homer's partiality to his own profession or more generally to reflect the admiration for the artist that is endemic in Greek culture from the beginning. But the request has its point in the plot. When the Phaeacian king Alcinous notices Odysseus's tearful reaction to the song of the Wooden Horse, he is prompted to ask him about his identity, which question leads naturally into the long narrative of Odysseus's wanderings from Troy.

It is **ironic** that the Trojan events in which Odysseus took part have now themselves become part of the bard's repertoire to be sung as an after-dinner entertainment. The phrase 'He took it up at the point where' suggests that the bard, whether we take him to be Demodocus or Homer himself, has the whole **saga** at his fingertips; within the tale the bard shows the same artistry about beginning as in the larger narrative. He begins in the middle of things or, more accurately, at a pivotal point of the action. He does not waste time telling us about the making of the horse or about the discussion by the Greeks of their plan, but comes to the critical point where the Trojans are debating about what to do with it. This has the simple effect of intensifying the irony when they make the decision to 'let it stand as a magnificent offering to appease the gods'. Unfortunately for them it proves to be a device which causes their destruction, thus appeasing the gods they have offended. This in turn emphasises what follows, that it was their destiny to perish by this device. The brief allusion to the presence of Athene at the making of the horse and her 'indomitable' presence alongside Odysseus when he is fighting Deiphobus underscores the feeling of a divinely supported fate both at Troy and in the action of the poem itself where Athene has been supporting Telemachus and has been present with Odysseus in Phaeacia.

The Wooden Horse was Odysseus's greatest stratagem as a result of which he could be called the man who sacked Troy (Book 1, lines 1–2) and so is suitably brought before the audience's mind to raise him in the imagination just before his identity is revealed. When he makes his request, Odysseus does so in such a way that certainly draws attention to his own role (false modesty is not an Homeric virtue) both in the clever device of the ambush, which he will repeat in the plot against the Suitors, and in his fierceness in carrying it out, for he fights like Ares the war god himself, as he will fight fiercely against the Suitors at the climax of the action. The mention of Menelaus, the husband of Helen whose abduction caused the Trojan War, and Deiphobus the Trojan who, according to later accounts, married Helen after the death of Paris, again puts Odysseus at the very centre of the Trojan story.

But in making his request he also has an interest in testing the accuracy of the bard's account. His reaction utterly vindicates the bard, who is able to induce a loss of self-control (from a hero normally most self-possessed) that he feels bound to conceal. His proneness to tears here shows him to be a sensitive hero, 'much suffering' and not hardened to suffering in the process. There is no triumphalism here.

This is very apparent in the extended **simile** in which the hero's copious tears are likened to the tears of a bereaved wife whose husband has fallen in battle, fighting for the defence of his city. This evokes not the Greeks who sailed overseas to right a wrong but the Trojans defending their city against the evil day. In fact it might remind readers of the *Iliad*, of Andromache mourning the dead Hector. In the brutal treatment of the woman by her enemies as she is led off into slavery is an unsentimental picture of the realities of war. The Trojan past in the *Odyssey* becomes a theme for the evocation not of heroic achievement but of suffering and regret. It might also be said that the narrative of 'many-minded' Homer characteristically extends sympathy and compassion to the defeated and does not gloss over the evil consequences of war. This simile is longer than it need have been and deliberately draws attention to itself beyond the immediate point of comparison, painting a vivid picture of suffering that goes beyond Odysseus's tears. Homer has sometimes been criticised for his 'long-tailed' similes. But the artistry of this one extends our perspective beyond that of the hero. Its effect is to emphasise the theme of human suffering (reflected in one of the recurring **epithets** of his hero: *polytlas*) and to make it universal.

TEXT 2 (BOOK 18, LINES 66–117)

They all approved his words, so Odysseus tucked up his rags round his loins and bared his fine massive thighs. His broad shoulders, and his chest and brawny arms were now revealed – Athene herself stood by and filled out the limbs of this shepherd of the people. As a result, all the Suitors were lost in amazement, and significant glances and comments were exchanged;

'Under those rags of his, what a thigh the old fellow has! Irus is going to be un-Irused. He was looking for trouble and he'll find it.'

Irus was badly shaken by these comments. But in spite of that the servants hitched up his clothes and dragged him forcibly to the front, though he was in such a state of panic that the flesh quivered on all his limbs. And now Antinous burst out with a tirade of abuse.

'You great ox! It would be better for you if you were dead or hadn't been born, if you are going to stand quaking there in mortal terror of an old man broken down by the hardships he's endured. I'll tell you this, and it will happen. If this fellow beats you and shows himself the better man, I'll throw you into a black ship and send you over to the mainland to King Echetus the Destroyer, who'll have your nose and ears off with his cruel knife and rip away your privy parts to give them as raw meat to the dogs.'

At these words Irus' limbs trembled all the more. However, they dragged him into the ring, and the pair raised their fists. The patient, good Odysseus considered carefully whether he should fell him with a mortal blow or knock him to the ground with a gentler punch. In the end he decided on the lighter blow, so that the Achaeans would not suspect him. Then they both drew themselves up. Irus aimed a blow at Odysseus' right shoulder, but Odysseus struck Irus' neck below the ear and smashed in the bones so that the red blood gushed up through his mouth and he fell down in the dust with a scream, grimacing and drumming on the earth with his feet. At this the noble Suitors threw up their hands and died of laughing. Odysseus seized Irus by the foot and dragged him out through the entrance across the courtyard to the portico gate. There he propped him against the courtyard wall, put his stick in his hand and said in words that flew: 'Sit there now and scare the pigs and dogs away. You're a worthless fellow, so don't try to lord it over strangers and beggars, or something worse will happen to you.' Then he slung the strap of his worn and shabby knapsack over his shoulder and, returning to the threshold, sat down again.

The haughty Suitors flocked back into the hall laughing gleefully and congratulated Odysseus. 'Stranger,' they said, 'may Zeus and the other gods grant you your dearest wish and your heart's desire for having stopped that glutton from roaming about the land. Now we'll soon pack him off to the mainland, to King Echetus the Destroyer.'

The noble Odysseus was glad of their unconsciously prophetic word.

Odysseus, disguised as a beggar, has already entered the palace and been insulted by Antinous, the Suitors' leader. He soon encounters the resident beggar nicknamed Irus (alluding to Iris, a messenger of the gods) since he was at everyone's beck and call. Irus tries to warn him off but Odysseus insists that there is room for both of them and warns him in turn that if it comes to a fight he will trounce him. Antinous sees what is going on as a source of entertainment. He offers a prize of two goats' paunches to the winner. Odysseus gets the Suitors to agree not to intervene on Irus's side. Telemachus speaks to ensure fair play. It is his words that are approved by all at the beginning of the extract.

As far as the Suitors are concerned, the fight between the two beggars is a comic affair, as is evident in their witticism about Irus being un-Irused and in their extreme reaction to his discomfiture when he is knocked down. They are still laughing when they re-enter the hall after having watched the stranger eject him. This part of the **epic**, because of its low and undignified subject matter, has sometimes been called comic by critics, but what for the Suitors is gratuitous fun is for Odysseus a serious test. He must maintain his disguise and this is part of his calculation in his decision not to kill Irus. All that happens too is a continuing test of the Suitors whose conduct here in their gross delight in an unseemly contest is a further breach of the high Homeric manners evidenced in the orderly and regulated households of Nestor (Book 3), Menelaus (Book 4) and the Phaeacians (Books 7–13). Odysseus himself, whatever the unseemly comedy surrounding him, conducts himself gravely, remains in control and continues to be a figure who retains the audience's respect throughout from the moment his physique is revealed beneath the rags to his moral pronouncement at the end.

There is a notable contrast in the insults offered to Irus first by Antinous and then finally by Odysseus. Antinous, whose name suggests someone who lacks understanding, simply hurls abuse with a crude threat that he will send him off to the mainland to King Echetus the Destroyer (who sounds like a bogeyman from folklore) where he will be subject to unspeakable barbarity. The motif is repeated at the end so the threat seems not simply to be verbal abuse, though we never find out whether it is carried out. However, though Irus is an unpleasant character there is no kind of justice in threatening him with such a punishment simply because he loses the fight. Odysseus's insult, on the contrary, is a just rebuke relating to his previous treatment by the swaggering Irus who had provoked him to the fight in the first place.

The disguise always entails piquant **ironies**. Here the Suitors' prayer at the end is doubly ironic. In the first place it is ironic in the light of their own profligacy and extravagant eating and drinking that they should complain of the gluttony of a beggar. But the greater irony, as the final line makes clear, is that they are unwittingly praying for their own destruction and that prayer itself is taken as an omen of that imminent destruction by Odysseus. The whole episode in fact proves to be prophetic of their own fate at the hands of Odysseus the Destroyer. In this episode as in the larger narrative his treatment of those around him is distinguished from theirs because it is just.

The effect of the contest is not simply comic, therefore; it is in various ways a jarring narrative and this is reflected in the language. For the most part, the language is direct, physical and low. The beggar's rags and his shabby knapsack are simply described. The insults are delivered

TEXT 2 continued

directly and the physical details of the fighting are specific and graphic without being in any way dressed up in evasive poetic language. Yet there are at points in the narrative epic **formulae** which seem to have an ironic ring in the context of this beggarly fight. When Athene fills out his limbs Odysseus is described in the formulaic phrase 'shepherd of the people'. When he contemplates how he should deal with Irus he is given two of his epithets *polytlas* 'much enduring' (here translated as 'patient') and *dios* 'godlike' ('good' here). He addresses Irus with 'winged words'. Finally the Suitors are given their habitual epithet *agauoi* glossed in dictionaries as 'noble' (perhaps because of their high birth) and so translated here once and as 'haughty' a second time. The formulae remind us that something is amiss. The Suitors are ignoble whatever status their birthright gives them. Odysseus is still much suffering, godlike and a shepherd of his people who speaks with authority despite the circumstances in which he finds himself. The jarring language underwrites the jarring thematic content.

TEXT 3   (BOOK 23, LINES 153–208)

Meanwhile the lion-hearted Odysseus, in his own home again, was bathed and rubbed with oil by the housekeeper Eurynome, and clothed by her in a beautiful cloak and tunic. Then Athene enhanced his comeliness from head to foot. She made him look taller and sturdier, and she caused the bushy locks to hang from his head thick as the petals of a hyacinth in bloom. Just as a craftsman trained by Hephaestus and herself in the secrets of his art takes pains to put a graceful finish to his work by overlaying silver-ware with gold, she endowed his head and shoulders with added beauty. He came out from the bath looking like one of the everlasting gods, and went and sat down once more in the chair opposite his wife.

'What a strange woman you are!' he exclaimed. 'The gods of Olympus gave you a harder heart than any other woman. No other wife could have steeled herself to keep so long out of the arms of her husband who had just returned to his native land after twenty wearisome years. Well, nurse, make a bed for me to sleep in alone. For my wife's heart is as hard as iron.'

'What a strange man *you* are,' said the cautious Penelope. 'I am not being haughty or contemptuous of you, though I'm not surprised that you think I am. But I have too clear a picture of you in my mind as you were when you sailed from Ithaca in your long-oared ship. Come, Eurycleia, move the great bed outside the bedroom that he himself built and make it up with blankets and brightly coloured rugs.'

This was her way of putting her husband to the test. But Odysseus flared up at once and rounded on his loyal wife. 'Lady', he cried, 'your words are a knife in my heart! Who has moved my bed? That would be hard even for a skilled workman, though for a god who took it into his head to come and move it somewhere else it would be quite easy. No man alive, not even one in his prime, would find it easy to shift. A great secret went into the making of that complicated bed; and it was my work and mine alone. Inside the court there was a long-leaved olive-tree, which had grown to full height with trunk as thick as a pillar. Round this I built my room of compact stone-work, and when that was finished, I roofed it over carefully, and put a solid, neatly fitted, double door. Next I lopped all the branches off the olive, trimmed the trunk from the root up, rounded it smoothly and carefully with my adze and trued it to the line, to be my bedpost. I drilled holes into it, and using it as the first bedpost I constructed the rest of the bed. Then I finished it off with an inlay of gold, silver and ivory, and fixed a set of gleaming purple straps across the frame. So I have shown you the secret. What I don't know, lady, is whether my bedstead stands where it did, or whether someone has cut the tree-trunk through and moved it.'

At his words her knees began to tremble and her heart melted as she realized that he had given her infallible proof. Bursting into tears she ran up to Odysseus, threw her arms round his neck and kissed his head.

After the Suitor-slaying, Eurycleia has told Penelope that her husband has returned and that she has recognised him from his scar. Penelope is not convinced, saying that it might be the work of a god. Telemachus has rebuked her for her hard-heartedness. Odysseus has set tasks for his son so that he can speak privately to his wife.

For the climactic reunion, Athene enhances his appearance. The **simile** of the hyacinth imparts beauty to his description and suggests the typical curled hair of later Greek statuary. The more extended simile that follows indirectly associates the hero with the gods; Hephaestus, as the cunning artificer, and Athene, goddess amongst other things of the mechanical arts, are appropriate deities in view of Odysseus's skill as a craftsman apparent in his account of the bed-making which is to follow.

The simile directly likens Athene's enhancement to the polish given to his work by a skilled and careful craftsman, in particular to his overlaying silver with gold. This enhancement of Odysseus by Athene is in fact similar to the enhancement given by Odysseus to his own craftsmanship in the making of the bed when he finishes it with an inlay of silver, ivory and gold. In both cases there is a typical Greek concern with a beautiful appearance. The line describing his emergence from the bath in its simple arrangement 'he rose from the bath in form like one of the immortals' provides a fitting visual climax; we can envisage Odysseus actually rising from the bath. A simple domestic action like taking a bath in preparation for a romantic encounter has become the occasion for enchanting visual poetry.

Face to face and alone, the conversation between Odysseus and Penelope is artfully managed. Odysseus's reproach that no other woman could have hardened her heart and remained aloof from her husband who has returned after twenty years indirectly draws attention to Penelope's great endurance and steely resolve during his long absence. That she does not immediately yield is surely a psychological master-stroke on the part of Homer. Her caution has been prepared for by similar scepticism on the part of Eumaeus and Telemachus. In her reply Penelope, who is here given her **epithet** *periphron* ('wise', 'thoughtful', here translated 'cautious') uses the same formulaic address to turn the tables on her husband. The word *daimonie*, translated as 'strange' here surely is apt for both parties after all that has passed. Her remark that she has too clear a picture of him as he embarked for Troy delicately allows recognition of the change he has undergone in twenty years and imparts a note of realism to this recognition scene that is perhaps lacking when the remarkably long-lived Argus, Odysseus's old dog, is supposed to recognise his master after twenty years' absence.

The test involving the bed is a further master-stroke. Penelope the wise is the only mortal to get the better of Odysseus. It is the kind of test that Odysseus himself might have devised and puts her on an equal footing with her husband. It produces a strong reaction in Odysseus who momentarily loses control. The bed is a physical bed, of course, but given that it is their marriage bed the prospect of its removal has implications that are not spelt out but nevertheless there in the final phrase 'whether someone has cut the tree-trunk through and moved it'.

The description of the making of the bed is very detailed, workmanlike and precise. Homer has sometimes been censured for passages like this which have been thought to be beneath the dignity of **epic** poetry. Epic poets after him often describe physical actions in general or summary terms or through the use of elegant poetical **periphrasis.** This is never Homer's way. He will call a spade a spade if it is necessary to include a spade in the detail of the action. The passage has relevance; the detail is needed for Odysseus to pass the test and convince Penelope that he is who he says he is. At the end of the description, almost as if he has realised that he is being tested, he tells Penelope that he has shown her the secret. Furthermore, it is an intimate secret known only to husband and wife (and a maidservant of whom we otherwise know nothing), so that it has the indirect effect of enhancing the intimacy of this scene as well as impressing the audience with another display of Odysseus's practical talents. Odysseus the wily man of wit takes obvious pride both in the secret of the bed and his own craftsmanship in the making of it. It therefore has a psychological credibility too. It also has its own attractiveness because of its visual clarity and the unusual interest of the picture it creates. Finally, in the narrative structure it allows time for Penelope to melt. The simple and direct expression of her emotion at the close comes as a release and change after the detailed demonstration and proof.

PART FIVE

Background

THE HOMERIC QUESTION

Nothing is known for certain about the authorship of the *Odyssey* or about its date and place of composition. Indeed all the circumstances surrounding the composition and early transmission of the Homeric poems are matters of surmise and controversy that together have come to be known as the Homeric Question. It is unlikely that a satisfactory solution to the problem that has perplexed scholars and critics alike in an acute form for nearly two centuries will now ever be found. The literature upon the subject is very considerable and all that can be done here is to indicate some of the main difficulties and to record the latest consensus of scholarly opinion. That consensus may be more apparent than real and at best can offer only a likely account.

The Homeric poems are the oldest surviving texts in Greek culture. There are no internal references to their author or to their origin and there are no other contemporary documents to throw light upon them. They exist in what is virtually an historical vacuum. Nor is there any reliable tradition about their origin in the earliest Greek literature following them. The Greeks all agree on the name 'Homer' and there is a persistent tradition that, like the bard Demodocus in the *Odyssey*, he was blind, but different views are recorded concerning his date and birthplace. Seven cities claimed to be the birthplace of Homer, the most favoured in antiquity being Chios and Smyrna, both in the region of Ionia in the eastern Aegean. The Greeks believed in the historical reality of the Trojan War, but they questioned the reliability of the Homeric version. According to some accounts he was a contemporary witness of events; according to others his poem was composed some time after the fall of Troy, an event which in any case was for the earliest Greek historians shrouded in the mists of prehistory.

Any consideration of the Homeric Question must begin with the picture of the Homeric bard in the *Odyssey*. There are two bards in the poem, Phemius, resident in the palace of Odysseus in Ithaca, and the blind Demodocus who resides in the palace of King Alcinous in Phaeacia which is visited by Odysseus in the course of his wanderings from Troy. Both bards have an honoured place and sing to the accompaniment of the lyre. Phemius sings of the woes inflicted on the Greeks returning from Troy (Book 1, lines 326–7). Demodocus sings three short songs, the first of which is about a quarrel between the leading Greeks at the beginning of the Trojan story (Book 8, lines 73–82). The second is a comic tale about the gods (Book 8, lines 266–366). The third is at the request of Odysseus, who commends Demodocus for his truthfulness in faithfully recording the memory of the sufferings of the Greeks at Troy and asks him to sing of the Wooden Horse, the stratagem by which the Greeks took Troy. Demodocus being stirred by the god of song begins from the point at which the Greeks sailed away (line 500). He tells how the Trojans took the huge horse into the city thinking that the Greeks had departed, and how the Greeks hidden inside it came out at night and sacked the city (Book 8, lines 487–520). The implication is that Demodocus knows many songs about gods and heroes and that in particular he knows the whole Trojan story which he can take up at any point. Moreover, the bard faithfully transmits the memory of the great events of the past. Later in the poem Phemius boasts to Odysseus that he is self-taught and knows many different songs. The poet of the *Odyssey* and the *Iliad* must be a descendant of the Homeric bard he describes. But Demodocus and Phemius work on a small scale with single tales. There is no hint in either the *Odyssey* or *Iliad* of an occasion which could have prompted the composition of poems of such great length and scope.

How could the poems have been transmitted? Early literary sources report the existence of a guild called the Homeridae who claimed to be the descendants of Homer, and who flourished in Chios and were devoted to the recitation of his poems. In addition, there were other professional reciters of Homer's poetry called *rhapsodes*. Their existence is well attested, and they recited Homer's poetry from memory at public festivals and games where they competed with one another for prizes. Again it is difficult to imagine an occasion on which the poems might have been recited in their entirety.

It was the lack of any known occasion for poems of this length, together with the difficulty of explaining how poems of this length and artistic unity could have been composed without the aid of writing, that led the German Homeric scholar Friedrich Wolf (1759–1824) to raise the Homeric Question. It is not that Wolf denied the existence of 'Homer'. He believed that Homer had existed and had initiated the poems in their early form. But he declared in his *Prolegomena ad Homerum* of 1795 that the Homeric poems, as we know them, did not have a single author but had progressively evolved, as successive *rhapsodes* added to and developed what had come down to them. Some ancient scholars, known as the *chorizontes* or separators, had believed that the *Odyssey* and *Iliad* were by different authors, and some ancient commentators had suspected that particular lines and even some episodes had been interpolated, but it was not until Wolf that unity of authorship in the individual poems was fundamentally questioned.

Wolf's theory arose primarily from a consideration of the external factors mentioned above. After him the poems themselves were rigorously analysed. Internal discrepancies and inconsistencies were seen to be evidence of multiple authorship. In this time even those who disagreed with Wolf's conclusions accepted that the Homeric poems had come into being gradually over a period of time, since it is apparent that like a rock face they contain various layers of material, some of which must be given a comparatively late date and some that belong to earlier time.

Archaeology & the Homeric Poems

The ancient Greeks had believed in the substantial reality of Homer's world but in modern times students of Homer from the eighteenth century onwards tended to believe that the material world of Homer and the events he described were poetic fictions, until in the later part of the nineteenth century archaeologists began to reconstruct the early history of civilisation in the Mediterranean from the physical evidence provided by excavations. The most famous name in Homeric archaeology is that of the German scholar Heinrich Schliemann (1822–90) who excavated what he believed to be the site of Troy at Hissarlik in northern Turkey in the early 1870s. His conviction that he had found Homer's Troy has not always been shared by subsequent archaeologists. He later excavated Mycenae in 1876 and Tiryns in 1884 on the Greek mainland. Other places mentioned in Homer, notably Pylos, were investigated by other archaeologists. Shortly after 1900 Sir Arthur Evans (1851–1941) excavated Cnossus in Crete, and these early archaeological endeavours provided the foundation for new knowledge about ancient Greece in the period before literary records are available. This new knowledge has tended to suggest that the culture and events of the Homeric poems have some basis in historical truth.

The island of Crete is the earliest centre of civilisation in the Mediterranean. The remains at Cnossus show that the Bronze Age civilisation called Minoan (from Minos the mythical lawgiver of Crete) was highly developed and lasted from roughly 3000 to 1000BC. On mainland Greece, a Bronze Age civilisation centred upon royal palaces such as those excavated at Mycenae, Tiryns and Pylos developed somewhat later and lasted from 1580 to 1120BC. This civilisation is called Mycenaean from what seems to have been its most powerful centre, Mycenae. In the *Iliad* Agamemnon, leader of the Greek expedition to Troy and the most powerful of the Greek princes, comes from Mycenae which Homer calls 'rich in gold', 'broad streeted' and 'well built'. In the catalogue of ships in the second book of the *Iliad* the largest numbers come from Mycenae and Pylos. The great house of the *Odyssey* bears a resemblance to Mycenaean palaces excavated on the main sites. The region in which the palace of Odysseus was located is thought to have been on the edge of Mycenaean civilisation. On both Thiaki, believed by the ancients and by many moderns to have been Homer's Ithaca, and on Leucas (now a promontory but possibly an island in remote antiquity), the other main rival for identification with Ithaca, there are Mycenaean remains.

A script known as Linear B on clay tablets found at Pylos, Mycenae and Cnossus establishes strong links between Minoan and Mycenaean civilisations, and the decipherment of the script in the 1950s established that their common language was an archaic form of Greek. The extant tablets record accounts and inventories that have to do with the routine administration of the royal palaces. How widely the script was known and used cannot be ascertained. There is no evidence that it was used to record literature. The script is, comparatively speaking, a cumbersome one, and could hardly have been used for a literary work of the length of the *Odyssey*, even supposing that suitable materials were available, such as leather or parchment. Nevertheless the existence

of the script is an indication of the developed material culture of
Mycenaean Greece.

After the destruction of Cnossus in 1400BC, Mycenaean civilisation
was at its most powerful and advanced. The most substantial remains
at Mycenae, the so-called Treasury of Atreus and the Tomb of
Clytemnestra (Atreus was the father of Agamemnon and Clytemnestra
was Agamemnon's wife) were built after 1300BC and the Lion Gate of
Mycenae (so called from the relief over its lintel) dates from 1250BC. The
fortification walls were mighty indeed. They were between twelve and
forty-five feet thick and it has been estimated that they were as high as
forty feet. The treasures found by Schliemann in the royal graves at
Mycenae, which include the famous gold face-masks, bear witness to the
opulent beauty of Mycenaean art work which was highly sophisticated in
its craftsmanship and design. The techniques of engraving, enchasing
and embossing were well developed and so was the art of inlaying bronze
with precious metals. Ivory and amber imported from the east and the
north are commonly found and indicate the extent of Mycenaean
commercial relations. Mycenaean pottery of this period is found widely
throughout the Mediterranean, a further indication that the Mycenaeans
were great sailors and traders.

Excavations at Hissarlik, the site of Troy, have revealed nine
settlements, the sixth settlement having substantial fortifications and
monumental walls. The seventh of these settlements was destroyed in a
great fire in the mid-thirteenth century BC, so that archaeological
evidence seems to support the possibility of an historical Trojan War of
which the Homeric account records the poetic memory. Soon after this
possible date for the fall of Troy, Mycenaean power began to decline,
until in about 1120BC Mycenae and Tiryns and with them the
Mycenaean culture of the Bronze Age were destroyed by the Dorians
invading from the north. The Dorians were themselves Greek-speaking
and possibly lived on the fringe of the Mycenaean empire. They initiated
what is usually known as the Dark Ages, lasting from 1100 to 800BC. The
Bronze Age gave way to the new Iron Age. Refugees from the dispersal
on mainland Greece created by the Dorian invasion now began to
colonise the eastern seaboard of the Aegean Sea known as Ionia in Asia
Minor. The Homeric poems are generally considered to have been
composed in Ionia (largely on linguistic grounds); they may therefore

preserve the memory of the Mycenaean mother culture transmitted by those who had colonised Asia Minor.

THE LANGUAGE OF HOMER

Historians of the Greek language have identified the same kind of layered structure as that revealed by the archaeologists, in which archaic elements exist side by side with later Ionic forms. The language of Homer is a fusion of elements from various dialects, the chief of which are the Ionic, the Aeolic, and the Arcadian. The predominant element is the Ionic, and this is the main reason for believing that the Homeric poems emanate from Ionia, but the Arcadian and Aeolic forms and vocabulary suggest that the Homeric epic has its roots in earlier times. The Arcadian and Aeolic dialects are descendants of dialects of Greek spoken in mainland Greece in the south and north respectively during the Mycenaean period. The fusion of these dialects with the Ionic has resulted in the view that Ionic bards took over and adapted to new circumstances and a new audience material that they had inherited from the past.

It is not simply a question of the fusion of different dialect forms and vocabulary which suggests that the language of the Homeric poems has a long and complicated history. Study of Homeric composition has revealed a highly sophisticated process at work which can only have been refined over a long period of time. The process involves the development and use of **formulae,** the stock in trade of the oral poet who composed without the aid of writing. Some recurring Homeric formulae have become world famous such as 'the wine-dark sea', 'rosy-fingered dawn' or 'winged words'. Formulae may be short phrases like the above or extend to longer passages describing oft-repeated actions such as putting out to sea, the preparation of a meal or the ritual of sacrifice. Formulae are convenient units that can be readily committed to memory and are therefore an aid to improvisation for the oral poet who is wholly dependent upon memory. In a famous study of Homeric formulae in the 1920s, the American Homeric scholar Milman Parry (1902–35) demonstrated both the scope and economy of the system of formulaic composition.

It is necessary to have some rudimentary knowledge of Greek metre and the structure of the Greek language in order to understand how the formulaic system works. Homer's metre is the **hexameter**, a metre of six units (called feet); it is an arrangement of long and short syllables according to fixed rules. Greek metre is quantitative, that is, words are fitted into the metrical pattern according to length of syllable. (In English metre the pattern is determined by accent, by the stress given to words in pronunciation.) The scansion of the hexameter is as follows:

$$- u\ u\ |-u\ u\ |-u\ u\ |-u\ u\ |-u\ u\ |--$$
$$-\ -\ \ |-\ -\ \ |-\ -\ \ |-\ -\ \ |\ \ \ \ \ \ |-u$$

A long syllable followed by two short ones (sounding like tum ti ti) is called a **dactyl** (hence Homer's metre is often known as the dactylic hexameter) and two long syllables together are called a **spondee** (tum tum). The first four feet may be either dactyls or spondees (with usually more dactyls than spondees). The fifth foot must be a dactyl and the final foot is never a dactyl, though the final syllable may be short, thus making a **trochee** (tum ti). This recurring rhythmical pattern at the end of the line in the fifth and sixth foot (a recurring tum ti ti tum tum or tum ti ti tum ti) creates a regular rise and fall and gives an effect not wholly unlike that of rhyme, though rhyme itself is never used in Homer nor indeed in any classical Greek or Latin poetry.

Greek is an inflected language so that the forms of nouns and adjectives change according to the particular case in question, whether nominative, vocative, accusative, genitive or dative. (In an inflected language there are naturally many similar sounds at the ends of words as adjectives have the same case as the noun which they qualify. This may account for the avoidance of formal rhyme schemes in classical literature.) Homer has a number of adjectives to describe the hero of the *Odyssey*. All these adjectives are generally appropriate to his character and role. But what Parry demonstrated is that in any particular context what governs the choice of a particular adjective is above all a metrical consideration. The various noun/adjective combinations (and sometimes there can be more than one adjective) all make different metrical patterns so that they can be slotted into the metre in different places. There are many combinations of noun and adjective for Odysseus. Each of these is determined by the case of the noun and by the position that the noun has in the verse, but no one of these combinations duplicates another; they are all metrically different. The scope is evident in the large number of combinations which have been developed to meet any syntactical and metrical need. The economy is evident in the fact that each of these combinations is unique, metrically speaking, and therefore allows the poet great flexibility in expression. Metre, of course, in any poetry determines what can and what cannot be said. What is remarkable about Parry's analysis of Homeric composition is that it suggests the restrictions inherent in oral composition and the extraordinary technical virtuosity through which they have been overcome.

The formulaic character of Homeric epic can explain how it is that there are various layers, the earliest of which transmit relics of Mycenaean times. The oldest linguistic elements are probably what have come to be known as the '**traditional epithets**', such as 'owl-eyed Athene', 'cloud-gathering Zeus' or 'Triton-born Athene', some of which perplexed the Greeks themselves. The first systematic study of Homer in the late sixth century seems to have been concerned with the need to explain obsolete and difficult words. The formulaic character also explains why Homer's adjectives occasionally seem inappropriate in their particular context, why, for example, Penelope's hand is described as being strong (Book 21, line 6). Finally, the formulaic character of the epic goes some way to explain the obvious fact of repetition. About one third of the lines in the *Odyssey* are repeated wholly or in part in the course of the poem. Equally one third is not made up of phrases found elsewhere. It is clear that the traditional inheritance was constantly being added to and varied to meet contemporary needs and the requirements of different tales. Homer's language, therefore, had been purposely developed for poetic recitation; it was never a spoken language. Nor did such a development, any more than the myths or the tales themselves, originate with one genius. There is a consensus of scholarly opinion that the language of the Homeric poems evolved over many centuries and that its technique of formulaic diction goes back to the Mycenaean age from which it was no doubt transmitted by practising bards like Demodocus and Phemius in the *Odyssey*.

Here the consensus stops and the Homeric Question remains. The poetic excellence of the Homeric poems presupposes individual talent. Nobody can believe that the lost tradition consists of countless poems of the quality of the *Odyssey* and *Iliad* which have not come down to us. Where does the individual talent stand in relation to the tradition? Most would say that 'Homer' came at the end of it. But was he a fully **oral poet** like Demodocus and Phemius, or did he use the oral method simply because he was composing for recitation? Did he dictate the text to a scribe, or did he write it himself? These are all open questions.

Comparisons with oral epics in other cultures show that, in preliterate cultures, feats of memory that would be considered astonishing in a literate culture are common enough. Bards have recited from memory, or have improvised poems, that are longer than the *Odyssey*. But such poems are comparatively crude and rarely have either the complex structure or the finished artistry of the Homeric poems. The difference in quality between the Homeric poems and oral epics in other cultures is as significant as anything that they have in common.

The problem is not made any easier by the inconclusive results of attempts to provide a date for the poems. The various layers that are apparent in the *Odyssey* have been so fused that neither linguists nor archaeologists have been able to unravel the puzzle. Most authorities envisage a date somewhere in the eighth century BC for the composition of the poems.

Nor is it known for certain when writing was introduced in Greece. Evidence suggests that knowledge and use of the syllabic Linear B script referred to earlier did not survive the fall of Mycenaean civilisation in the late twelfth century BC. Sometime between the tenth century and the eighth a new alphabetic script from Phoenicia was adopted in Greece. Papyrus (a form of paper originating in Egypt) seems not to have been introduced until later. Leather is known to have been used for writing quite early, though it would have been a costly business to commit a poem the size of the *Odyssey* to leather. Any kind of book is a rarity until the fifth century BC. Nevertheless, the materials were available and it is theoretically possible that the poems were committed to writing at an early stage.

The earliest written text of Homer for which there is any evidence in Greek sources dates from the late sixth century BC when the Athenian leader of the day is reported to have brought texts of the poems to Athens and to have required the *rhapsodes* who recited Homer's poetry at the annual Athenian festival to do so one after another in proper order, so that the poem would be recited as a whole. Given the special status of Homer in Greek culture from the earliest times, attested in the formation of special guilds of *rhapsodes* to recite the poems, it is certainly credible that there was a need for a definitive text.

The first textual criticism of Homer was carried out in the third and second centuries BC at Alexandria in the famous library there, by a succession of scholars, the most notable of whom was Aristarchus (*c*.215–145BC). Many texts of Homer had been collected for the Alexandrian library, and divergencies in the number of lines and variations in wording were glaringly apparent. At this time the Homeric text was standardised, and each poem was split up into twenty-four books, each given a letter of the Greek alphabet and a title heading still used to this day. This text standardised at Alexandria is the ancestor of all the texts that have come down to the modern world.

The Alexandrian version was copied, like other ancient texts, on papyrus rolls until the late second century AD when the codex (a book with pages) was introduced and papyrus was gradually replaced by more durable parchment. The oldest surviving complete manuscripts are medieval, but fragments of the poems on papyrus survive from Graeco-Roman times. Some manuscripts preserve the opinions of the ancient commentators and the notes of Alexandrian textual critics in the form of **scholia**, comments written in the margins above and beside the text. Similar material is also incorporated in compilations made by Byzantine scholars from collections of material now lost. The most notable of these compilations is the vast commentary on the poems made sometime in the twelfth century by Eustathius, Archbishop of Thessalonika. These Byzantine commentaries, the scholia and ancient papyri have all been used by modern textual critics to arrive at the best possible text of the Homeric poems.

PART SIX

CRITICAL HISTORY & FURTHER READING

GREEK RESPONSES

THE EARLY ALLEGORICAL TRADITION

When, early in the intellectual development of Greece, the first philosophers challenged the view of the world represented in the Homeric poems, attacking the theology and sometimes the morality of Homer, his defenders resorted to **allegorical** interpretation, identifying beneath the literal surface meaning of Homer's words and fictions undermeanings (*hyponoiai*), which conformed to later notions about the nature of things. The story of Ares and Aphrodite told by Demodocus (Book 8, lines 266–366) can be allegorised (somewhat fancifully) as follows. Hephaestus represents pure thought, which is static, so that he is lame. Ares and Aphrodite, representing strife and love, are caught and disciplined by the divine artificer. The gods laugh because they are really assisting Hephaestus in the creation of the universe. Many of the earliest allegories were physical. Allegorical interpretation was well established by the time of the philosopher Plato (*c.*427–348BC), who mistrusted it on the grounds that it is the literal meaning that makes the impression, and he believed that in their obvious meaning the Homeric poems misrepresented the nature of the divine and encouraged wrong attitudes and opinions about life. He therefore banished Homer from his ideal Republic, believing the poems to be a bad influence upon the young. After Plato there were countless defenders of Homer, who sought to prove in their commentaries that under the veil of fiction Homer was really a good philosopher.

According to the traditional interpretation of the allegorisers, Odysseus, because of his wisdom, is able to enjoy pleasure, but does not become a slave to it: he masters Circe, makes her his friend and sleeps with her without danger to himself. The episode becomes a lesson in temperance rather than abstinence. The Lotus-eaters and the Sirens represent different forms of the seductive temptation to hedonism and irresponsibility. In the Cyclops we see basic human savagery, the state of nature in which the individual will is not controlled and civilised by the social bond. In the main action the defeat of the greedy Suitors, representing only excess and appetite, is accomplished by the man of control who uses his intelligence. This kind of interpretation can be reductive, of course; even the figures in the fabulous wanderings are presented in a more human way than this flat account of them suggests. Polyphemus, for all his cruelty, is nevertheless very fond of his favourite ram. But these undermeanings sometimes suggest underlying themes, implied meanings or archetypal patterns and help to explain the perennial appeal of the poem.

'Allegoria' in Greek simply means saying one thing in terms of another, and the sense in which it was used by the Greeks was not altogether precise. Homer tells us at the beginning of the *Odyssey* that the hero has incurred the wrath of Poseidon, that he is in the power of Calypso, a nymph who lives in a cave on a desert island. In Book 5, Zeus sends Hermes to free the hero from her clutches. In Book 1, Zeus tells us that he had sent Hermes to Aegisthus to warn him that Orestes would come and take vengeance if he attempted to usurp Agamemnon's throne. Later allegorists explain that Homer means that most of Odysseus's troubles come from the sea, that he has been living for seven years on a paradise island in hidden pleasure (Calypso in Greek means the Concealer) until reason asserts itself through the prompting of the mind. Similarly Aegisthus knew perfectly well, when he thought about it, what the consequences of his action would be. Not all the allegories are therefore absurd. When a modern cultural historian tells us that in archaic Greece Homer did not know how to represent psychological change without the use of the supernatural – that when, for example, Athene puts *menos* (strength) into Telemachus we are to interpret this as his way of showing that the youth summoned up the necessary inner resolution to face the Suitors – he is a descendant of these early allegorists.

HOMERIC PROBLEMS & QUESTIONS

Homer has not been without his critics, and from earliest times adverse judgements have been made about aspects of his art. In antiquity books were produced of Homeric problems, in which problems were raised and solutions discussed. Some of the problems and criticisms were niggling and silly, reflecting the philistinism of those who made them. Such hypercriticism is associated with the name of Zoilus, a critic of Homer living in the fourth century BC. Others raised genuine problems which have since become part of the larger Homeric Question. What were earlier seen as artistic weaknesses or oddities have lately come to be regarded as points of evidence against unity of authorship in the argument of analytical critics. A representative selection of the commonest points that have been debated about the *Odyssey*, most but not all having a possible bearing upon the Homeric Question, and some of them of the niggling kind, is listed below in an order suggested by the arrangement of the poem itself.

- The relevance of much of what passes in Books 1–4 (The Telemachid) has been questioned, as has the wisdom of Homer in delaying the appearance of his hero until Book 5.
- Much depends upon the fact that Telemachus has just come of age. Eurynome remarks that he is now a 'bearded man' (Book 18, line 176). Yet Odysseus has been away for twenty years, so that Telemachus must be over twenty.
- Does the folk motif of the web (first mentioned by Antinous at Book 2, lines 96–122) violate the realistic spirit in which the events of Ithaca are represented?
- In comforting Penelope, why does not Athene reveal to her the whole truth (Book 4, lines 836–7)?
- Zeus declares that Odysseus must journey to Scherie without divine guidance (Book 5, line 32) yet Poseidon intervenes (Book 5, line 282) and Odysseus is helped by Ino, a water nymph (Book 5, line 351) and by Athene (Book 5, line 382).
- Odysseus covering himself with leaves is likened to a thrifty man on an outlying farm who keeps his fire alive under black ashes (Book 5, lines 488–90). Does this **simile** demean the hero of the poem? Homer has been much criticised for his low images, particularly in similes. Earlier Odysseus had been likened to a cuttlefish (Book 5, lines 432–3). The most notorious is the comparison of the restless state of the hero to a black pudding being tossed to and fro over a fire (Book 20, lines 22–7).
- Is Nausicaa immodest in saying that Odysseus is the sort of man she could marry (Book 6, line 244)?

- Why does Odysseus fail to answer Arete's question about his identity (Book 7, line 238)? Why is she given such prominence in the Phaeacian episode?
- What is the relevance and propriety of Demodocus's song about the illicit love of Ares and Aphrodite (Book 8, lines 266–366)?
- Going ashore on the island of the Cyclopes, Odysseus decides to find out what sort of people live there, whether brutal or god-fearing (Book 9, lines 175–6). He then has a foreboding that he is about to meet a being of enormous size (Book 9, lines 213–14). Is the episode well linked to the rest of the poem, or is the stitching whereby the folktales of the deep sea yarns and the surrounding narrative are knitted together too obvious? Can the representation of Odysseus in the episodes, as the man who desires to see things for himself, be reconciled with the view we have of him in the main action as the hero who longs to return home?
- How just is the accusation of Eurylochus that Odysseus shows reckless folly in leading his men into dangers in which they lose their lives (Book 10, lines 431–8)? If it is true, is it not damaging to the integrity of the hero either as a wise man or as one who is prudent and can be master of any situation?
- Book 11 in its present form has been regarded either as a late interpolation in its entirety (is the overall design and effect of the poem impaired without it?) or as a later expansion of an original Homeric core. In Book 8, Odysseus's instant departure is foretold (Book 8, line 150). In Book 9, he breaks off his narrative to announce that it is time to go to bed, and the Phaeacians press him to stay another day. This has been said to be a flimsy connection. Odysseus witnessed the death of Elpenor yet asks his spirit how he died. It has been argued that there are two conceptions of Hades. In the Minos scene (Book 11, line 575 onwards) the ghosts appear to have their faculties intact, whereas in the rest of the narrative they can only regain consciousness after drinking blood. Although Odysseus is above ground initially, it appears that he is actually in the underworld itself at points in the narrative when he is observing the activities of the ghosts. Not all that is described seems relevant to the poem. What is the point of the catalogue of women? What is the relevance of Elpenor and his fate?

- Homer has been censured on the grounds of implausibility for allowing Odysseus to be deposited in Ithaca asleep.
- The pace of the poem slackens in Book 13. Not all readers have felt that the Ithacan narrative is well planned or well paced. Are all the stories told in Eumaeus's hut necessary, and, if so, is the narrative not too long? These scenes involving characters from low life have been thought more appropriate to comedy than to epic. In particular the device whereby Odysseus elicits a cloak from Eumaeus (Book 14, lines 459–518), the encounter with Melanthius (Book 17, lines 212–54), the fight with the beggar (Book 18, lines 1–116), the play on Irus's name (Book 18, line 6), the various jokes and raillery of the Suitors (for example, Book 18, lines 351–5 and Book 20, lines 292–8) have all been censured as violations of **epic decorum**.
- The character of Theoclymenus has puzzled commentators, who have questioned his role in the poem. His history is given at length (Book 15, lines 223–56) yet he plays little effective part other than as an augur who foresees the Suitors' death (Book 20, lines 351–7).
- The episode involving the recognition of Odysseus by his dog Argus has been censured on the grounds of lowness (the mention of realistic details like the dunghill or the dog's fleas being a violation of epic dignity), improbability (the dog must have been over twenty years old with a very long memory) and sentimentality (Book 17, lines 290–327).
- In a clear manoeuvre, Odysseus arranges that he should be washed by Eurycleia (Book 19, lines 335–48). It then occurs to him that she might recognise him by the scar (Book 19, lines 388–91). Is this bad strategy on the part of Odysseus and/or Homer? The long account of the incident in which Odysseus received the scar has been censured as a pointless digression (Book 19, lines 393–466).
- Penelope decides to institute the contest with the bow just at the moment when she has had a number of indications from different sources that Odysseus is about to return. Telemachus has told her that Odysseus is still alive (Book 17, lines 142–6); both Theoclymenus (Book 17, lines 152–61) and the stranger (Book 19, lines 303–7) have prophesied his return. Is her decision adequately and credibly motivated?
- Is the killing of the Suitors noble and heroic, brutal and primitive or just fanciful and incredible?

- There seems to be confusion in the plans to remove armour from the hall. Odysseus at Book 16, lines 281–98 tells Telemachus to remove all but two sets which are to be left in a handy position nearby. In the event Telemachus goes down to the storeroom where he picks out four sets (one each for their two helpers). What is to be made of this apparent contradiction (Book 22, lines 108–10)?
- The punishment of the maids has been censured for being unnecessarily barbaric (Book 22, lines 437–73).
- In the recognition scene Penelope has been criticised for her stubbornness, scepticism and caution, and Odysseus for his coldness and hard-heartedness. Is the scene psychologically convincing?
- Homer's Byzantine commentator Eustathius preserves the verdict of Aristarchus that the Homeric *Odyssey* ended at Book 23, line 296 when Odysseus and Penelope retire to bed. Analysts have regarded the present ending as a late addition, pointing to the following anomalies. Hermes is nowhere else in Homer seen in the role of *psychopompos* (Book 24, lines 1–10). The White Rock is a puzzle (Book 24, line 11). The unburied Suitors enter Hades (the usual belief is that due burial rites are required before the spirit can pass to the underworld). Agamemnon and Achilles appear to meet for the first time (Book 24, line 24). Amphimedon thinks that Odysseus prevailed upon Penelope to arrange the contest with the bow (Book 24, line 167). This has been thought to be inconsistent with the actual narrative. No good reason can be found for the lies that Odysseus tells his father, or even for their meeting at all.

ARISTOTLE & LONGINUS

In his *Poetics* (*c.* 340 BC), Aristotle is mostly concerned about tragedy but he has scattered remarks on Homer that have become famous (see Chapters 8, 17, 23 and 24). Given the shaping influence of Homer on Greek art and culture, it is hardly surprising that, in his comments on unity in a work of art, his touchstone is Homer. He points out that a work of art does not have a unity simply because it deals with one character, because many different things happen to a character that do not necessarily make up a unity. Homer, whether through instinct or knowledge of his art, knew this when he did not put into the *Odyssey* all that happened to Odysseus, but made the poem cohere in a single action (Chapters 8 and 23). He points out that the actual story of the poem is quite short (giving a brief summary in Chapter 17); its expansion comes from the episodes. He remarks that while the *Iliad* is a simple story turning upon calamity (the Greek word is *pathetikon*), the *Odyssey* is complex, being full of discoveries (*anagnorisis*) and turns on character (*ethike*) (Chapter 24). We might add that a further source of complexity is the point of departure in the middle of things and the use of retrospective narrative.

In the treatise *On the Sublime* attributed to a Greek rhetorician named Longinus (of uncertain date), Homer is a frequent touchstone exemplifying the sublime or the grand in style. Most of Longinus's examples are from the *Iliad* which he regarded as the more sublime. In fact his comparison of the two poems, in which he seems to use Aristotle's distinctions, has become famous. He judged the *Odyssey* with its penchant for narrative and romance inferior to the *Iliad* with its vigorous action and 'strong tide of motions and passions'. 'I spoke of the *Odyssey* [which he regarded as a product of Homer's old age] only to show, that the greatest poets when their genius wants strength and warmth for the pathetic, for the most part employ themselves in painting the manners. This Homer has done, in characterising the Suitors, and describing their way of life; which is properly a branch of comedy, whose peculiar business it is to represent the manners of men' (Chapter 9, line 15). Later, the idea that, in the *Iliad*, Homer was the father of tragedy, while in the *Odyssey*, with its depiction of the manners of men and its happy ending in which the principle of poetic justice is upheld, he is the father of comedy became a commonplace.

Don Cameron Allen, *Mysteriously Meant: The Rediscovery of Pagan Symbolism and Allegorical Interpretation in the Renaissance*, Baltimore, 1970
Contains a chapter on allegorical tradition relating to the *Odyssey*

Howard Clarke, *Homer's Readers*, University of Delaware Press, 1981
Contains a substantial chapter on 'Homer Allegorised'

David Dawson, *Allegorical Readers and Cultural Revision in Ancient Alexandria*, University of California Press, 1994
A study of the various schools of allegorical interpretation in antiquity

T.S. Dorsch, translator, *Classical Literary Criticism*, Penguin Books, 1965

Contains Aristotle's *Poetics* and Longinus's *On the Sublime*

Robert Lamberton, *Homer the Theologian*, University of California Press, 1986

A systematic study embracing Greek and Christian allegories

TRANSLATION & REWORKINGS

Translation may be regarded as a form of interpretation that itself may involve a critical assessment of the original, and Homer has been much translated. The two most famous English versions are those of George Chapman (*c.*1559–1634) published in 1616 and Alexander Pope (1688–1744) published in 1726. Chapman's is a highly allegorised rendering in which Odysseus triumphs over his external enemies not merely through his superior wisdom but also by his own conquest of his self. He 'confesses' past weaknesses before the Phaeacians and rededicates himself to the domestic virtues. Pope largely dispensed with allegories and produces a vigorous rendering but still with a strong moral emphasis.

The difficulties faced by Homeric translators, particularly of the *Odyssey*, are memorably expressed by Matthew Arnold in his *Lectures on Translating Homer*:

> the translator of Homer should above all be penetrated by a sense of four qualities
> of his author: – that he is eminently rapid; that he is eminently plain and direct,
> both in the evolution of his thought and the expression of it, that is, both in his
> syntax and in his words; that he is eminently plain and direct in the substance of
> this thought, that is, in his matter and ideas. ... And yet, in spite of this perfect
> plainness and directness of his ideas, he is eminently *noble*; ... This is what makes
> his translators despair. 'To give relief' says Cowper [William Cowper (1731–1800)
> who translated Homer in the late eighteenth century] 'to prosaic subjects' (such as
> dressing, eating, drinking, harnessing, travelling, going to bed), that is to treat such
> subjects nobly, in the grand style, 'without seeming unseasonably tumid, is
> extremely difficult'. It is difficult, but Homer has done it. Homer is precisely the
> incomparable poet he is, because he has done it. His translation must not be

tumid, must not be artificial, must not be literary; true; but then also he must not be commonplace, must not be ignoble.

Two famous modern works alluding to the Homeric original are the modern novel by James Joyce, *Ulysses*, published in 1922 (The Bodley Head) and the long verse narrative *Omeros* by the Caribbean writer Derek Walcott, published in 1992 (Faber).

George Chapman, *Chapman's Homer*, edited by Allardyce Nicoll, Volume Two, *The Odyssey*, Routledge & Kegan Paul, 1998
A reissue of this standard edition

George de Forest Lord, *Homeric Renaissance: The Odyssey of George Chapman*, Chatto & Windus, 1956
A scholarly exposition of Chapman's relation to the allegorical tradition

H.A. Mason, *To Homer Through Pope: An Introduction to Homer's Iliad and Pope's Translation*, Chatto & Windus, 1972
Contains a chapter on modern translations of the *Odyssey*

Alexander Pope, Translations of Homer: The Odyssey, edited by Maynard Mack (Volumes IX and X *The Twickenham Edition of the Poems of Alexander Pope*, general editor, John Butt), Methuen, & Yale University Press, 1967
Contains not only the text but Pope's notes which form an extensive commentary

Robin Sowerby, 'The Augustan Odyssey', *Translation and Literature*, 4.2
An essay on Pope's *Odyssey* in the light of its contemporaneous reception and Matthew Arnold's later criticism of it

W.B. Stanford, *The Ulysses Theme: A Study in the Adaptability of a Traditional Hero*, 2nd edition, Basil Blackwell, 1963
A study of representations of Odysseus through the ages

George Steiner (ed.), *Homer in English*, Penguin Books, 1996
An excellent wide-ranging anthology of translations and adaptations of Homer from Chaucer to the present

R.H. Super (ed.), *Matthew Arnold: On the Classical Tradition*, University of Michigan Press, 1960
Contains his lectures 'On Translating Homer'

LANDMARKS IN THE HISTORY OF HOMERIC INTERPRETATION & CRITICISM

In the long period of Homeric reception there are three epoch-making moments springing from the *Prolegomena ad Homerum* of Friedrich Wolf (1795), written in Latin (no English translation is available), from the archaeological discoveries of Heinrich Schliemann made in the 1870s and the theories of Milman Parry concerning the oral composition of the poems in the early 1930s. Their contribution is briefly described in Background.

Wolf formulated 'The Homeric Question' with a clarity that forced it to general attention. The attempt to answer it generated a vast and daunting literature on the subject over the next 150 years. Although no satisfactory answer has been given or is ever likely to be given, it will not go away and continues to haunt Homeric studies.

If we look back now on the arguments of the analysts, those who use what they regard as discrepancies in the poems to argue for multiple authorship, what may seem striking is their overrationalistic approach. Often they are expecting the kind of logic in construction and connection that might be appropriate for the classic realism of nineteenth-century novels, designed to be read, but which is not appropriate for poems designed for dramatic oral recitation. Similarly Shakespearean scholars sometimes make much of discrepancies in his plays that would not, indeed could not, be noticed in a production. 'Unitarians', those who believe in the essential unity of the poem's authorship, have sometimes been able to turn their arguments round by arguing that, far from disclosing evidence of multiple authorship, these discrepancies reveal the skill with which the Homeric bard blended material from different sources. Nevertheless, the work of the analysts, particularly when it involves linguistic considerations, cannot be dismissed. In the case of the *Odyssey*, they have argued that the second strand of the double plot, involving Telemachus, is a later addition by a poet who had scruples about the original story in which Odysseus simply reasserts his rights over his own house. The Suitors' plot to kill him, of course, puts them unambiguously in the wrong and makes this reassertion doubly just. They have also found evidence of two versions of the ending. In a clear manoeuvre, Odysseus arranges to be washed by Eurycleia who nearly gives the game away. Then we see Penelope soliciting gifts from the Suitors with Odysseus's secret approval. It is certainly likely that in another version Odysseus took Penelope into his confidence and that this was a pre-arranged plan. The arguments are still of great interest because, where they do not depend absolutely on linguistic considerations, they involve debates about narrative art in which any reader may join and out of which may come a heightened critical awareness. Moreover, the question of the poem's composition cannot be simply put to one side. Our sense of what it is cannot be divorced from our sense of what went into its making. And our judgement of the finished product will depend upon this sense.

The oral theory of Parry, backed up by the evidence of the observed and recorded practice of orally improvised composition in modern Yugoslavia, and continued by his pupil Albert Lord, goes a long way to explaining the obvious fact of repetition of lines and indeed whole passages containing typical themes such as the arming of the hero or the making of a sacrifice. The singer is not an original genius but more of a skilful mechanic. They stress the degree to which the singer works within and manipulates a traditional inheritance of predetermined formulae and in a sense does not or indeed cannot say anything new. This determinism may seem obviously to overstate a case, since reason requires that formulae come from somewhere, but it emphasises the degree to which Homeric composition is shackled by metrical considerations and further raises difficult questions about the relation of the individual singer to the tradition.

The impasse surrounding the Homeric Question has not prevented other researches into the Homeric background. Whether or not Schliemann was right in his conviction that he had found the site of Troy, later archaeology has uncovered physical evidence that suggests that the poems have a firm grounding in the culture of the Bronze and Iron Ages of Greece. Convinced that the poetic fiction overlays a kernel of historical reality, later historians and social anthropologists have sought to use the poems to locate the social customs of early Greek society (sometimes using comparative knowledge of other early social systems) and then used the picture so constructed to illuminate the poems. Since there is little other direct evidence, this is to some extent a circular move, but there is no doubt that to read the poems through such an anthropological perspective is helpful and worth while. For instance in *The World of Odysseus*, M.I. Finley works on the assumption that the poems, whatever connection they have with the Mycenaean world, emanate from a later and more insecure time, the last stage of a period when Greece was governed by petty kings. He gives a detailed assessment of the assumptions and customs upon which such a social system existed and shows their relevance to a full understanding of the *Odyssey*, illuminating, for example, the issues surrounding the absence of the king and the position of his wife and the underlying economic organisation of the royal household.

In the last two decades, the study of literature has been increasingly influenced by new waves of theoretical criticism emanating from continental Europe and the United States. So far this has made little impact upon Homeric studies, which may seem surprising, given the scholarly attention paid to these foundation texts in the western tradition. In very general terms, it might be said that one aim of much modern theory is to unsettle comfortable notions about 'original genius' (often regarded as a bourgeois illusion), about the relation of an artist's work to his life and about the relation of the artist's life to the times in which s/he lives. But since Wolf's *Prolegomena*, nobody has had any comfortable notions about the authorship of the Homeric poems or their relationship to the culture that produced them. Modern critics have sometimes talked of 'the death of the author'. Homer, as an author, died two centuries ago. Another aim of modern theorists, whose starting point is the limitation of language as a self-referential system, is further to undermine the autonomy of the self-directed artist. Since Parry, Homeric scholars have been only too well aware of the limitations imposed on the artist by the traditional language system in which he works.

The great question-mark hanging over these productions has had an inhibiting effect, so that it is not merely that the world of classical scholarship has been slow to catch up with modern thinking, more a case, perhaps, that much modern thinking about literary production and the relation of art to society and of the artist to his inherited linguistic medium has already been anticipated in the mainstream, even if the discussion has not been conducted in the same terminology.

Howard Clarke, ed., *Twentieth Century Interpretations of the Odyssey*, Englewood Cliffs, N.J., 1985

A useful collection containing a variety of comment for the general reader

Howard Clarke, *Homer's Readers: A Historical Introduction to the Iliad and Odyssey*, University of Delaware Press, 1981
> An admirable compilation of responses to the poems with chapters on the early romance tradition, Renaissance criticism (much of it hostile), the allegorising of Homer, the debate between analysts and unitarians, and the contributions of archaeologists, oral theories and anthropologists. This sets out in the clearest terms the various approaches, debates and arguments about the poems

M.I. Finley, *The World of Odysseus*, Penguin Books, 1962
> An historian's estimate of the social reality implied in the poems

Albert. B. Lord, *The Singer of Tales*, Harvard University Press, 1960
> A disciple of Parry, who relates the Homeric poems to the compositions of contemporary Yugoslav oral poets

T.H. Myers, *Homer and his Critics*, edited by Dorothea Gray, Routledge & Paul, 1958
> A general survey, emphasising history and archaeology

Milman Parry, *The Making of Homeric Verse*, edited by Adam Parry, Oxford University Press, 1971
> Parry's ground-breaking theory of the oral formulaic character of Homeric verse composition

T.B.L. Webster, *From Mycenae to Homer*, Praeger, 1958
> Relates the poems to Bronze Age Mycenaean culture

FURTHER READING

WORKS OF GENERAL REFERENCE

Atlas of Ancient and Classical Geography, Everyman's Library, J.M. Dent, London, 1950
> Includes a map of the world as it seems to be represented in Homer

A.J.B. Wace & F.H. Stubbings, eds, *A Companion to Homer*, Macmillan, 1962
> A standard authoritative work introducing many areas of Homeric scholarship

Michael Grant & John Hazel, eds, *Who's Who in Classical Mythology*, Weidenfeld & Nicolson, 1979

Simon Hornblower & Anthony Spawforth, eds, *The Oxford Classical Dictionary: The Ultimate Reference Work on the Classical World*, 3rd edition, Oxford University Press, 1996

M.R. Scherer, *The Legends of Troy in Art and Literature*, Phaidon Press, 1963

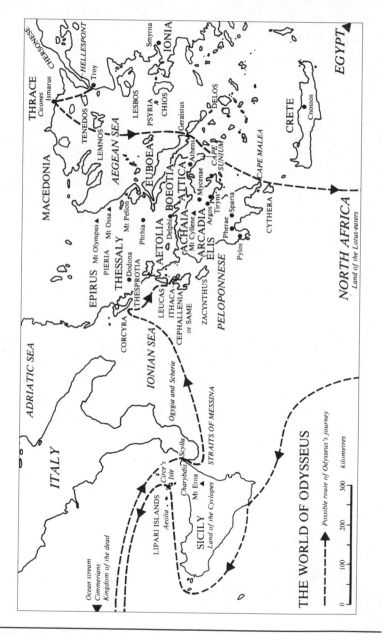

THE WORLD OF ODYSSEUS

– – – – Possible route of Odysseus's journey

kilometres

0   100   200   300

CHRONOLOGY

Many dates are approximate and frequently disputed

⊚ Ancient Greece   ● Culture   ⊚ World events

BRONZE AGE

⊚ 3000-1000BC Minoan civilisation
centred on Crete

⊚ 2870BC First settlements at Troy

⊚ 1900BC Bronze Age begins in Britain

● 1860-1500BC Stonehenge

⊚ 1580-1120BC Mycenaean civilisation
centred at Mycenae on mainland Greece

⊚ 1556BC Kingdom of Athens begins

⊚ 1546BC Kingdom of Troy founded

⊚ 1450BC Zenith of Minoan civilisation

⊚ 1400BC Destruction of Cnossus, the capital of Crete

⊚ 1250BC Destruction of Troy

● 1230BC Exodus of Israelites from Egypt

IRON AGE - DARK AGE

● 960BC Solomon builds temple
in Jerusalem

⊚ 776BC The first Olympic Games

⊚ 750BC Greek alphabet
on Phoenician model

● 750BC Homeric poems

● 610-580BC (c) Sappho, Greek poet

● 600-500BC (c) Buddha Gautama lived

● 535BC (c) Evidence that Homeric poems were
put in order to be recited at Athenian festival

● 509BC Foundation of Roman Republic

CLASSICAL AGE

⊚ 490-322BC Classical period in Greek civilisation –
democratic government

⊚ 490BC Greeks defeat Persians at the battle of Marathon

● 479BC Death of Confucius

⊚ 445BC Herodotus reads his *History* to Council of Athens

● 406BC Deaths of Euripedes and Sophocles,
Greek dramatists

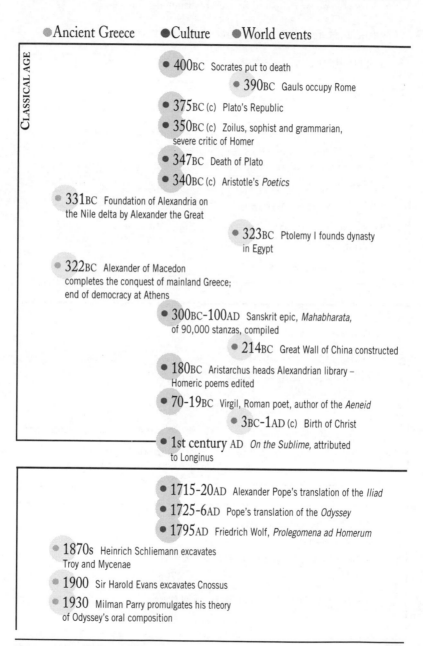

Ancient Greece   Culture   World events

CLASSICAL AGE

400BC   Socrates put to death

390BC   Gauls occupy Rome

375BC (c)   Plato's Republic

350BC (c)   Zoilus, sophist and grammarian, severe critic of Homer

347BC   Death of Plato

340BC (c)   Aristotle's *Poetics*

331BC   Foundation of Alexandria on the Nile delta by Alexander the Great

323BC   Ptolemy I founds dynasty in Egypt

322BC   Alexander of Macedon completes the conquest of mainland Greece; end of democracy at Athens

300BC-100AD   Sanskrit epic, *Mahabharata,* of 90,000 stanzas, compiled

214BC   Great Wall of China constructed

180BC   Aristarchus heads Alexandrian library – Homeric poems edited

70-19BC   Virgil, Roman poet, author of the *Aeneid*

3BC-1AD (c)   Birth of Christ

1st century AD   *On the Sublime,* attributed to Longinus

1715-20AD   Alexander Pope's translation of the *Iliad*

1725-6AD   Pope's translation of the *Odyssey*

1795AD   Friedrich Wolf, *Prolegomena ad Homerum*

1870s   Heinrich Schliemann excavates Troy and Mycenae

1900   Sir Harold Evans excavates Cnossus

1930   Milman Parry promulgates his theory of Odyssey's oral composition

allegory in Greek means saying one thing in terms of another and is used rather loosely in connection with Homer. Athene, the goddess of wisdom, might be regarded as an allegorical expression of the power of reason

catastrophe a change of fortune either way, not necessarily from good to bad. The catastrophe in the *Odyssey*, the killing of the Suitors, brings about a change from adversity to prosperity for the main characters

coda a concluding passage, usually in a musical context

dactyl a metrical unit or foot, comprising a long syllable followed by two short syllables (sounding like *tum ti ti*)

decorum fittingness, appropriateness; as a literary term it can refer to the appropriateness of character to plot, of language to character or of imagery to theme, or any combination of these, or the appropriateness of form and content, or content to genre (in this case epic). It is a key principle of classical art, admirably embodied in the Homeric poems, though parts of the *Odyssey* (e.g. the king disguised as a beggar or the 'lowness' of the similes) have sometimes been censured as violations of the decorum held necessary for epic

deus ex machina in Greek drama, the use of a god to tie up the loose ends of the plot, descending on to the stage by way of a 'machine'. By transference the term has been applied to use made of Zeus in his intervention at the close of the poem in which he declares peace

divine machinery a collective noun for the gods and goddesses, so called from their use as plot devices or mechanisms. Homer starts the *Odyssey* by means of a council of the gods. The plot is kept going through the agency of Athene and the opposition of Poseidon and concluded by Zeus at the end

double plot a two-stranded plot (the journey of Telemachus and the return of Odysseus), more integrated than a plot and subplot

dramatic irony when the audience knows more than the characters, occasioning many ironies. We know that the stranger in disguise is Odysseus

epic a work of art (usually a poem) on a grand scale, written in a grand style with heroic figures involved in a great tale or adventure; the *Odyssey* is a defining type of the genre with a unified plot diversified by numerous episodes, and such features as divine machinery, set speeches, formal epithets and extended similes

episode a part of the poem that is self-contained and not absolutely necessary for the main plot, e.g. the episode with the Cyclops

epithet the Greek word for adjective (derived from the Latin); used of the regular adjectives describing persons, places and things e.g. 'rugged' Ithaca, 'much enduring' Odysseus

formula recurring units of sense, repeated phrases (see Background, on The Language of Homer)

genre a distinct kind of literature, such as epic here or comedy or detective fiction, with its own conventions and characteristics

hexameter from the Greek word for six (hex) and the word for measure (metron); the metre of the Homeric poems and of all later epic poetry in antiquity

homily a sermon-like discourse intended to be edifying

irony saying one thing that has another meaning or implication

metaphor from the Greek 'carrying over'; one thing is described as being another, thus 'carrying over' all its associations, e.g. Telemachus and Odysseus accuse Penelope of having a heart of iron, where iron is not literal but metaphorical, carrying all the associations of this hard unyielding metal

oral poem one composed by improvisation for recitation (i.e. not by means of writing to be read)

pathos from the Greek, meaning strong emotion and often suffering

periphrasis the Greek word for circumlocution, that is talking around a thing rather than directly naming it, e.g. 'finny tribe' for fish; this example is not found in Homer who is sparing of periphrasis. A phrase like 'The king of the gods and men' may be regarded as a dignified periphrasis for Zeus

picaresque from the Spanish *picaro*, rogue; often applied to novels recounting a series of adventures featuring a likeable rogue

poetic justice a state of affairs when the good are rewarded and the bad punished, so called because it seldom happens in life, only in fiction

rhapsode literally a stitcher of songs; in ancient Greece used to denote the minstrels who performed parts of the Homeric poems, perhaps stitching together songs from various sources

saga a series of stories about a particular hero; the plot of the *Odyssey* comprises various elements from the saga of Odysseus about whom there were doubtless many stories

scholia explanatory or interpretative comments written around the text of the poem in manuscript versions of it

simile a comparison, often extended in Homer and a chief source of poetic imagery

spondee a metrical unit or foot comprising two long syllables (sounding like *tum tum*)

symbol something which represents something else by analogy or association, e.g. a sword representing war

trochee a metrical unit or foot comprising a long syllable followed by a short syllable (sounding like *tum ti*)

unity of action a series of actions linked by a probable or necessary chain of cause and effect, as in the main plot of the *Odyssey* involving the return of Odysseus and his re-establishment of order in his own house

AUTHOR OF THIS NOTE

Robin Sowerby was educated at St Catharine's College Cambridge, where he read Classics and English. He now lectures in the Department of English Studies at Stirling University. He is also the author of York Notes on *The Iliad*, *The Aeneid* and *The Republic* and Advanced Notes on Shakespeare's *Antony and Cleopatra*, *As You Like It* and *Alexander Pope: The Rape of the Lock and Other Poems*. He has edited selections from Dryden and Pope and is the author of *The Classical Legacy in Renaissance Poetry*, Longman, 1993 and *The Greeks: An Introduction to their Culture*, Routledge, 1995

York Notes Advanced

Margaret Atwood
Cat's Eye

Margaret Atwood
The Handmaid's Tale

Jane Austen
Mansfield Park

Jane Austen
Persuasion

Jane Austen
Pride and Prejudice

Alan Bennett
Talking Heads

William Blake
Songs of Innocence and of Experience

Charlotte Brontë
Jane Eyre

Emily Brontë
Wuthering Heights

Angela Carter
Nights at the Circus

Geoffrey Chaucer
The Franklin's Prologue and Tale

Geoffrey Chaucer
The Miller's Prologue and Tale

Geoffrey Chaucer
Prologue To the Canterbury Tales

Geoffrey Chaucer
The Wife of Bath's Prologue and Tale

Samuel Taylor Coleridge
Selected Poems

Joseph Conrad
Heart of Darkness

Daniel Defoe
Moll Flanders

Charles Dickens
Great Expectations

Charles Dickens
Hard Times

Emily Dickinson
Selected Poems

John Donne
Selected Poems

Carol Ann Duffy
Selected Poems

George Eliot
Middlemarch

George Eliot
The Mill on the Floss

T.S. Eliot
Selected Poems

F. Scott Fitzgerald
The Great Gatsby

E.M. Forster
A Passage to India

Brian Friel
Translations

Thomas Hardy
The Mayor of Casterbridge

Thomas Hardy
The Return of the Native

Thomas Hardy
Selected Poems

Thomas Hardy
Tess of the d'Urbervilles

Seamus Heaney
Selected Poems from Opened Ground

Nathaniel Hawthorne
The Scarlet Letter

Kazuo Ishiguro
The Remains of the Day

Ben Jonson
The Alchemist

James Joyce
Dubliners

John Keats
Selected Poems

Christopher Marlowe
Doctor Faustus

Arthur Miller
Death of a Salesman

John Milton
Paradise Lost Books I & II

Toni Morrison
Beloved

Sylvia Plath
Selected Poems

Alexander Pope
Rape of the Lock and other poems

William Shakespeare
Antony and Cleopatra

William Shakespeare
As You Like It

William Shakespeare
Hamlet

William Shakespeare
King Lear

William Shakespeare
Measure for Measure

William Shakespeare
The Merchant of Venice

William Shakespeare
A Midsummer Night's Dream

William Shakespeare
Much Ado About Nothing

William Shakespeare
Othello

William Shakespeare
Richard II

William Shakespeare
Romeo and Juliet

William Shakespeare
The Taming of the Shrew

William Shakespeare
The Tempest

William Shakespeare
Twelfth Night

William Shakespeare
The Winter's Tale

George Bernard Shaw
Saint Joan

Mary Shelley
Frankenstein

Jonathan Swift
Gulliver's Travels and A Modest Proposal

Alfred, Lord Tennyson
Selected Poems

Alice Walker
The Color Purple

Oscar Wilde
The Importance of Being Earnest

Tennessee Williams
A Streetcar Named Desire

John Webster
The Duchess of Malfi

Virginia Woolf
To the Lighthouse

W.B. Yeats
Selected Poems